COUNTRY TALK

COUNTRY TALK

JAMES PRESTON

First published in Great Britain 1985
by David & Charles (Publishers) Limited

Published in Large Print 2001 by ISIS Publishing Ltd.
7 Centremead, Osney Mead, Oxford OX2 0ES
by arrangement with David & Charles (Publishers) Limited

British Library Cataloguing in Publication Data
Preston, James, 1913–
Country talk. – Large print ed.
1. Country life – Great Britain
2. Natural history – Great Britain
3. Large type books
I. Title
941′.0858′092

ISBN 0–7531–9702–2 (hb)
ISBN 0–7531–9703–0 (pb)

Printed and bound by Antony Rowe, Chippenham and Reading

CONTENTS

Which way, Amanda, shall we bend our course?
The choice perplexes. Wherefore should we chuse?
All is the same with thee. Say, shall we wind
Along the streams? or walk the smiling mead?
Or court the forest glades? or wander wild?
Among the waving harvests . . . ?

*"Summer" from "The Seasons" by John Thomson,
author of the words of "Rule Britannia", and
published in 1727.*

CHAPTER
ONE

The Last Rabbit

We sat in the evangelist's tent listening to the canvas slapping the poles in the wind and counting the dulled marks where the cow-pats had been removed from the grass.

Cow-pats. The heavy sweet smell of cattle which dragged the memory back to the sick room; the sweet smell of old ladies dressed in black, dying of boredom in built-up beds in downstairs rooms in cottages which looked out distantly at other cottages looking out distantly . . . The sweet smell of trampled grass.

Running down a steep coombe we were knee-high in a mist of bluebells, perhaps unvisited in a century, and our feet trampled wild garlic. For a moment we stood in the timelessness of a new experience. There was only birdsong and broken light under oaks which had stood there since Saxon sheep grazed those downs. We walked on another ten miles — time and distance had no meaning in our childhood — but we never told anyone about the bluebells or the smell of wild garlic.

"We shall now sing hymn number seventy four . . ." The evangelist's voice was raised above the slapping of the canvas; his head was raised and circled, haloed, ennobled with a crown of thick grey hair and his name was Mr Bucket. "Mr Walter Bucket . . .?"

Hymn seventy four promised a form of exquisite punishment not to be found in hymn seventy three or hymn seventy five. But we were not for punishing. Not us, the keepers of secrets, not those who discovered, by accident, that adders could not climb out of paper bags. Why should we want paper bags when we were only going up to the Sea Mark on the downs? An empty paper bag on a thousand acres of open downland was an obvious incitation to mischief.

The blatant possession of an empty paper bag is sometimes difficult to explain to a parent. But the next day the answer was found. "Could we have some sandwiches for lunch?" The sandwiches, each an inch and then something thick and with nothing memorable inside them, were eaten by the time we got to the end of the lane. We always ate everything as soon possible. We carried all our meals inside ourselves; it left the hands free . . .

Coming back from the downs at the end of the day we still had the paper bags. They were full. Adders are stupid. You can creep up to them on children's feet and in a moment they really were in the bag. The secret seemed to be to catch them while they were asleep in the sun, grab them just below the head, but you soon learned and painfully, too, not to try to catch them while they were moving. There were a hundred adders below one hedge and all we had to do was to catch a few each.

Walking up the village's one street we offered Pauline a plum. With the innocence which only comes from a

2

girl who seemed to spend most of her life calculating ways of getting us boys into trouble, she said yes and she opened the bag.

Did you guess? Of course. She screamed. She ran. There were consultations between parents and we were beaten. It was much more fun being beaten than being promised the indefinable punishments of hymn seventy four.

"We love and adore thee . . ." No, we count the bleached patches where the cow-pats once rested; green and bubbly and smelling of cow's breath.

"Our hope and salvation . . ." Our curiosity that the evangelists should pitch their tent in that steep field above the brook, in the field in which it was reputed there were mushrooms. There was even a notice nailed to the ancient gate which warned trespassers — an open invitation to sin — that prosecutions would, in anticipation of hymn seventy four, be instant and profound.

And each morning, as soon as September started yellowing the grasses, the field was a moving festival of hope as men strolled, noses downwards, through the grass looking for mushrooms which were not there. We circled each other, watching all the other people in the field rather than looking for mushrooms. They had tea towels or cloths in the bottom of their baskets to cover the mushrooms they pretended they had collected. Then the game started.

"Hey," my cousin Charlie shouted. "Look at this one." It wasn't one. It could not be one, there had not been a horse in that field in living memory and we knew that

COUNTRY TALK

the magic of mushrooms was entirely dependent on the
benign presence of horses. The fictitious mushroom was
pulled from the grass and was put with a flourish of the
hand into the paper bag from which the adders had been
evicted.

The mushroom men were on us in seconds, elbowing
and shoving, pushing us boys out of the way. Even now,
thirty and then some years later, I can remember the
pinched face of a man saying to us that there was a
notice on the gate forbidding the gathering of
mushrooms in that field, but he, he had permission from
the farmer to be there. He would tell the farmer about us
and then there would be trouble and weren't we always
in trouble and now had we not invited even more trouble
upon ourselves . . .

We went and found other non-existent mushrooms in
distant corners of the field and in the seven acre field
next door and they still came running, elbowing and
shoving and pushing and telling us to clear off home.
Going out when the game was over, over the five barred
gate — we never went through a gate when we could go
over it, under it, round the ends or between the bars —
the man with the pinched face, pointing at the awful
warning of retribution to come, the friend of the farmer,
the man in slub flannel trousers, grabbed the paper bag
and said, "Let's see how many mushrooms you boys got
in that bag then?" Solemnly we opened the bag and
showed him . . . an adder.

Coming down the hill towards the brook on other days
we would see him. He would lean back against his

4

fence: "Liars. Little liars. Liars," he intoned as we went past.

We smiled but never spoke to him, and ever afterwards in the eternities of summer we could recite quietly to ourselves, "Liars, Little liars. Liars." Sometimes, wobbling by on his creaking bike he would get it wrong: "Little liars, liars, liars . . ." and we would shout the liturgy back in the correct order.

That was part of the imponderable of being a child. Hymn seventy four promised an indefinable punishment to the body after the body had ceased to exist. But was it possible to tell lies about mushrooms — which were not there? The mistake made by the evangelical church was in forgetting that children are born with an inherent comprehension of metaphysics and that eternal damnation wore slub flannel trousers and told lies.

But others believed Mr Bucket's message. She sat at the organ and worked the foot bellows with stockinged legs which would have looked proud on a crow. Her hair was tied in buns over her ears and each bun was carefully wrapped in a hairnet thick enough to catch pilchards. But the triumph of her musical ability was an announcement, made by Mr Bucket, who appeared to us to receive special instructions from high above the field in which mushrooms did not grow, to tell all seven of us in the mission tent, that the scatty old crow who played the organ was stone deaf. It was announced as a victory of religious fervour over physical disability.

At the end of hymn seventy four we applauded her deafness and Mr Bucket turned her round, a wild-eyed and bewildered Beethoven to face all seven of us — five adults and two small boys with grazed knees and grubby hands and faces which betrayed their amoral instinct of what had gone wrong. Hymn seventy four had been sung to the tune of another hymn. But it did not matter: Mr Bucket stood with his Bible clasped high to his left breast, his right finger pointing to the name of an Eastbourne tent-maker printed in stencil on the canvas roof, his voice louder than everyone else's, carrying above the sound of the peddle organ, above the sound of the wind slapping canvas and into the silence of the countryside and singing the wrong words ... to the wrong tune.

"Mr Bucket," I said going back up the hill in gathering darkness. "Mr Bucket."

"Mr Lavatory Bucket?"

"Yes, Mr Lav Bucket was singing the wrong words, wasn't he, to the wrong tune?"

"Little liar," Charlie said. "Liar, little liar, liar."

And as children always are, we were overheard calling Mr Bucket a liar and we were beaten. Worse, we were beaten and then heard through the floorboards the adults talking about it and laughing. We lay in the lumpy beds and listened and then Charlie said, quietly and with authority, "Never mind, tomorrow's Sunday and we have to go to Chapel".

Sunday was the only day of the week with a name. It was also the only day of the week in which we were not allowed to roam. We were not allowed to roam because we had to go to Chapel in the morning at 10.30. There were always eleven of us in the congregation, give or take a bout of 'flu, exept in the week when Mr Bucket and his tented mission was in the mushroom field. There were seven of us at his morning service; the same seven who attended the afternoon service, the same seven who attended the evening service from Monday to Saturday. On the following Sunday night, helped with our willing hands, the tent was packed, the peddle organ was loaded into the van and Mr Bucket and Mrs Bucket, who always looked at her husband slightly sideways as if she was trying to guess what he would do next, and the loopy peddle organist were packed inside and left for another part of the Island.

My aunt scanned the weekly newspaper to follow Mr Bucket's evangelical joy-ride round the Isle of Wight. Brighstone, fortunately, was too far away for us to visit him even once. The thought never seemed to cross anyone's mind that if Brighstone then was even smaller than Havenstreet and if Havenstreet could only muster seven hopefuls of salvation, how many could a small and scattered community like Brighstone provide? The answer was revealed by the proverbial lynx-eyed local reporter who put her greying head round the slapping canvas and did a quick count: no one.

There was Mr Bucket, bible to breast, finger to tent-maker; there was Mrs Bucket in a state of slight puzzlement and there was the loopy organist bashing Ancient, Modern and yet-to-be-dreamed-of out of the peddle organ and Mr Bucket was singing hymn seventy four . . . you can fill in the rest of the words yourself; wrong tune, wrong words . . .

This did not surprise us; near Brighstone, at least at that end of the Island, was a Chapel which had the

7

legend, "Primitive Wesleyan" carved over the façade. Now that sounded like a religion which could appeal to boys. But the Chapel was never open. The door was firmly locked, probably still is to this day. "Are you in there God?" we would shout through the letterbox. No reply.

"What are 'Primitive Wesleyans'?" Charlie asked.

"Don't ask silly questions." Roughly translated that meant, "We don't know."

"What do 'Primitive Wesleyans' do?" We hoped they danced about in the nude, shrieking and laughing and drinking light ale from the bottle; the women's great pink flanks heaving in ecstasies undreamed of in ordinary Wesleyan chapels, their great bosoms like sacks of potatoes wobbling with the passions of joy never promised in our Chapel and without the torments, damnations, threats of torture, pain, grief and anguish of the tented mission.

We climbed over the spiked railings and walked through the long grass that smelled of un-opened cupboards in old ladies' houses; wakened black cats with white bibs and, at the back, amongst the anonymous gravestones, found a city of voles. We looked through the clear-glass windows, they were primitive enough not to have invented stained glass, and discussed whether we should shout, "Come out, God, it's safe now. The mission has gone home to Eastbourne . . ." But the ghosts of heaving pink flanks and bosoms like sacks of potatoes remained as silent as God himself.

One day my aunt told us that we were going on a visit to St Helens. On a hot summer afternoon when we should, by rights, have been constructing another dam across Blackwater Brook, or smoothing the cold blue clay across the our naked bodies in the pool down by the heronry, we went on a bus to Ryde and then on a bus to St Helens. Buses are not as interesting as walking to St Helens across country.

The bus stopped at the apex of the green, my aunt got off, a light shining in her eyes, her round body caparisoned in a black summer overcoat secured with a single button, her whole self projected like an ambulatory missile towards, yes, you guessed, Mr Bucket's tented mission for the saving of souls, for the putting of the fear of God into miserable sinners. Yes, there was Mr Bucket, Bible in hand and clasped to the breast; there was the deaf peddle-organist with legs like a redshank's and there were the three of us in the congregation singing hymns, saying prayers and listening to sermons. There were five hymns . . . all sung to the same tune . . .

Boys came to the door of the tent and peered into the gloom and then mooched away to do what village boys do best. If either of us turned round we got a punch in the kidneys. Real Primitive Wesleyan that was. The hot sun beat down, the boys came and went and at each coming and going a feeling of deeper embarrassment and greater shame covered me.

"Look down, O Lord, upon James, miserable sinner that he is . . ."

Don't bother, Lord. James was only miserable at being in that tent and certainly he was not a sinner. Boys are amoral, not immoral. To err is human, to sin divine ... And I made up my mind that I would not again be embarrassed in the presence of the Almighty and I would avoid the arrogance of the man with the halo of grey hair and the tightly clasped Bible, to ask for salvation for myself or to hope that by standing in a field cleared of cow-pats I would create a private relationship with God.

The next time I was invited to "Join hands with Jesus", I politely declined and my aunt went off on her own to Chapel, and I never went again although I have a fairly good working arrangement with God now.

"The heron has four eggs," Jakie said. We did not believe him. He would appear occasionally and make such pronouncements. He was not one of us. Sometimes he would be with us for half a day or even a whole day. Then he would disappear. He was not a lonely boy, he was utterly isolated in his own thoughts. You could not get in; he had no desire to get out.

We walked down the hill towards the brook. Everything started at the brook. If you did not know what to do with yourself you went to the brook and sat under the bridge and thought about it. Usually the answer came long before you got to the brook and inquiring legs took us off elsewhere. If it rained we sat under the bridge and watched the rain boring holes in the water. We heard the cows tramping over the bridge, we heard the gentle chuffing of the trains in Havenstreet station and we learned the great mysteries of life.

The bus came twice a day to Havenstreet. It came down the hill at 3.30 in the afternoon and at 3.30 in the afternoon the gate of the farm near the White Hart would open and slow moving guernseys would turn, sweet-smelling as ever, hocks mud-caked, towards a distant field. The farmer walked behind the herd with his hand on the flank of the last cow and the herd moved at the pace of the slowest, udder-swinging cow.

Sometimes the bus hooted and the driver shouted out of the window. "Come over, lovely," Mr Butcher said, caressing the quarters of the guernsey with his hazel stick. "Come over, my lovely." But his lovely came not over. Nor did any of the others.

He caught us coming out of the mushroom field one morning. There was only one formal exit and he was leaning on it. We came sheepishly to the gate expecting our daily dose of trouble.

"Find any mushrooms, you nippers?" he said. We showed him the empty paper bag. "Didn't think so," and he pushed his cap back revealing an un-weather beaten bald head. We wondered whether he wore his cap in bed . . .

"Didn't think you'd find any mushrooms there, nippers," he said. "Aint none there, that's why."

"But why the notice on the gate?" we asked.

"My brother, he bought some mushroom spawn, must have been 1938 or so. Sowed it, he did, and do you know what happened?"

"No," we said eagerly. We were warming to Mr Butcher. Until that day we believed Mr Butcher had a secret accord with the world: he would not talk to the world and the world would not talk to Mr Butcher. It was a finite agreement which suited Mr Butcher very well. It also suited Mrs Butcher who not only did not speak to the world but did not speak to Mr Butcher either.

"No, what happened?" we asked.

"Didn't grow," Mr Butcher said. "Not one mushroom; never not one. Silly bugger." Mr Butcher walked back up the hill laughing to himself. "Silly bugger," he kept repeating, "never not one."

"Mr Butcher," we asked, because this really was the most important question, perhaps even the key to the universe, "Why do you always turn out the cows as the bus is coming through..?" The words were dying in our mouths as we said them. Mr Butcher looked at us with clear, unseeing eyes. He stood in silence, gazing at us for a long, long time before turning and shutting the world out of his yard. Had he forgotten his concordat with the world? Had he opened his mouth and spoken too much? Was Mr Butcher secretly a Primitive Wesleyan fighting a solitary war against the Southern Vectis Omnibus Company Limited, trying to disrupt their vital time-table on the single-decker route to Newport? We never discovered. Mr Butcher never spoke to us again. But we had learned a new phrase, "Silly Bugger". It was a lovely phrase. It slipped happily off the tongue at every inconvenient moment.

"How many eggs has the heron got?" we asked Jakie.

"Four," he said cautiously.

"Silly bugger," we said in unison. We fell back into the grass and sniffed elder. You cut elder with your pen knife. With a hard twig you could push out the pith to make a pea-shooter, or, if you were very clever, a whistle which played a single, thin note. Or, quite simply, you stripped the rough bark and revealed the white wood and the unique stench of elder. It was smooth and sensual to touch.

We could always see the heronry from a distance. The herons poised over the clump of ash trees on the bend of the brook, their great grey wings like feathered parachutes, motionless in the air for just one moment before dropping on the edge of the nest where they paddled their match-stick legs making sure that the nest they had themselves built was secure.

We stood underneath the nest, but not directly underneath. The branchless trunk of the ash for the top twenty feet was white-washed with heron's droppings. The ground at our feet was spattered with droppings, the air was still and filled with the sickly smell of fish, eaten, dropped, regurgitated for chicks ... Jakie took off all his clothes and then, slowly, his arms and legs grasping the bulk of the tree, climbed. Slowly only for the first thirty feet, then faster as the limbs narrowed. The parent herons stood on the edges of their nests, twice the size of dustbin lids, and looked down on the climbing boy with the same button-eyed, fixed stare as they looked into streams for roach or sticklebacks or in the high field where a row of them, solemn as magistrates, guzzled frogs in a silent ditch.

But when Jakie was ten feet from the top of the ashes the herons opened their beaks and it came out as a stream of white and grey vomit, of part digested fish, usually regurgitated for their young who poke their beaks into their parents' throats to have that rich meal passed lovingly from parent to child. Jakie got it all, unlovingly.

For a moment he stopped. The stenching mass which ran over him smelled beyond words. We retreated to the clear and moving air. Then, even more slowly, clearing the mess from the boughs Jakie climbed higher. How high? Sixty feet? How could we guess? One small boy in an ash tree so high he could sit in the top spread and put a hand through the torment of twigs at the base of the nest and raise one grey and white fluffed squawker for us to see. The noise of the herons flying overhead was like crows agitated to desperation. They turned, they swooped downwards on wide silver wings and Jakie, who felt the magic of love for herons that grown men feel for women and dogs, climbed quickly downwards.

He lay naked in the brook, the white mess floating slowly down on the never ending tide.

"Do you know," he said lying motionless in the water, "From up there you can see the yachts in Wootton Creek."

"Silly bugger," we said and Jakie smiled, lying naked, floating in the blue-muddied water.

"It's too high church," my aunt said as she cooked another vast breakfast for us, the only meal she could be sure we would have together, possibly on the grounds that it might be the last meal we would ever have

14

together although she never expressed for one moment any interest as to where we had been the previous day, or any inquisitiveness as to where we were going today. In any case we did not know where we were going until we had got to Blackwater Brook. What concerned my aunt more than the cooking of breakfast was that the liturgy of the church was too high.

We considered this perversion of the truth as we swung endlessly on the unoiled chains of the swings in the "recreation ground", a square, featureless paddock with foot-high clumps of grass, shapeless holes filled with builders' sand and two swings. We recreated ourselves frequently there, especially when feeling punchy against a hostile world which had beaten us once too often that week and which practised a liturgy which baffled my aunt for being too high.

We discussed at endless length the fact that a boy named Sambrook — a "Silly Bugger" name if ever there was one — had come to live in the village. He lived in a house with a clipped hedge and a fence and a gate which opened and clasped closed. Such orderliness was an open invitation to our peculiar, rural violence.

Charlie did not have a gate to his house. It had disappeared a long time ago. Most of the fence had also faded away, probably onto the sitting room fire, so that incontinent dogs of no known ownership peed nonchalantly on the ragwort in the front garden. That was reason enough to beat Sambrook with our clenched fists so that he went home in tears. That would teach him to live in a house with a gate and to attend church,

Mrs Sambrook wearing a hat and probably clean underwear . . .

My aunt met Mrs Sambrook and expressed great joy that a boy had arrived in the village to play with Charles. Mrs Sambrook drew herself up to her full and handsome height and said, "No thank you", with Hellenic fortitude, and we were henceforth never troubled again by participation in the liturgy of the high church.

But the bashing of Sambrook about the head did not entirely solve the problem of the high church. It was not so much a problem we could not solve, it was a definition we could not understand. The church was not high; it was low, it was squat and grey and inside it was peaceful and serene. It had a bellows organ which Charlie elected to pump — he was going through a mercenary stage — with a long wooden handle, and all this for 6d a week plus 6d for weddings and funerals when he was not at school. There were about four weddings a year and his income did not create much excitement as Jakie and I ate the sweets it bought.

There was also a reservoir measured by a lead weight which moved as the air depleted and rose as the bellows were pumped, and there was a point which only appeared by long experience below which the organ faltered and wheezed and went flat as a spinster's breast. The secret was to live dangerously and pump like fury when the weight reached . . .

. . . Except for the day when Charlie pumped the organ and a howl in no way related to the chosen psalm of the holy day wobbled from under the bellows. Why should a bitch sneak into a church and hide under the organ bellows? Was she in pup? The Rector and congregation gathered around the organ; the Rector sent for a slice off the Sunday joint to entice the bitch ... but by the time the mongrel appeared it was too late to start the service; too many Sunday lunches were in danger of burning. The Reverend Rompost stood on the altar steps, his stomach started just below his chin, his chins reached down to his chest, his altar boys were at his side but no incense had been burned that morning, no bells rung in that Church of England, and he roundly damned the least of God's creatures which for misery or loneliness or pain or for one of one hundred thousand reasons never to be revealed to us had crept for sanctuary under the organ until it had been disturbed by an unwashed, sixpence a week boy who pumped the organ.

We concluded, swinging endlessly on the unoiled chains of the swings, that the high church had a deep-rooted hatred of mongrels. Therefore, and this was a conclusion beyond further question or debate, we were not high church men ourselves, although if the question of mongrel bitches were to be reconsidered ...

Jakie lived in a gothic cottage at the edge of a distant lane which did not lead anywhere in particular. In whichever way you looked there were no other cottages, no other people. The landscape was mapped by rows of elms on the edges of lanes which crossed that greensand plain like veins on the back of your hand. Oaks, flat-topped, told the antiquity of the hedge and ash, grown for farm use, interspersed. We spent a lot of time simply looking at hedges, especially in the blackberry season. It was a Georgian landscape without overhead wires.

Jakie's parents regarded him with a remote curiosity, wondering amongst themselves how he came to be living in their cottage and whether they had a responsibility to feed him and clothe him or send him to school. They rarely did any of these things and spoke of him in the third person because they were not sure who he was and they never discussed him in public and he, like us, was left entirely alone in thirty square miles of countryside to find his own way in the world.

When we went back to the heronry Jakie had built a sacking hide in a neighbouring tree, in branches four inches wide, sixty feet above the ground, which swayed like a sailing ship in the evening breeze. He told us, rashly, that he left his money and his binoculars in the hide. "It's quite safe," he said with alarming truth. "No one else can climb that tree."

But in this conversation Jakie revealed another fundamental scientific fact never for one moment harked upon by Galileo or Leonardo never bought by the riches of Lorenzo the Magnificent; which was that if you crouched down and put a pellet of moist white bread into your bottom and made wind, the pellet shot across the room like a miniature cannon ball.

Not only had Jakie discovered this truly astounding fact, he had also, quite by the accident of being a solitary boy, found that he had a limitless ability to make wind. He could do it to order. He could recognisably play the first few bars of "God Save the King". We stood to attention when he did it. But best, best by far, was the fact that he could propel a morsel of bread six feet across his bedroom. We measured the distance with a box-wood ruler and declared it a World and Olympic record.

But there was one final act which needed waiting for: we waited with impatience in his bedroom. There was not much to contain interest, a single iron bed on an uncarpeted floor, a single chest of four drawers and a coat hanger on a hook behind the door. If you had a hide sixty feet up an ash tree in the heronry you did not need much at home.

As darkness filled the room, Jakie crouched in the familiar firing position, his skinny pink buttocks facing upwards, and with a Swan Vesta ready lit and held two inches from ... and then, like a shooting star in the night sky, a blue flame projected and in less than half a second faded into nothing.

"Do you think," Charlie said as we walked the three miles up the dark lane to home, "Do you think that Jakie is high church?"

CHAPTER
TWO

Village Summer, Village Winter

The telephone kiosk came late to our village and for reasons of unknown perversity was placed in the geographical centre of the village and not where the greater part of the population lived. Until that time, well after the war, we had a telephone shaped like a daffodil and with a piece you held to your ear.

Even when it arrived it was not connected to an automatic exchange. A young village woman plugged up the calls as they came in and, as a boy, if I wanted to speak to my father she would quickly tell me he was not at home. She would also tell me where he was going and what he was going to do when he got there.

The point about the village public telephone was that the operator blatantly listened-in to everyone's conversations. It was not that she was poking her nose into other people's affairs, but was an essential part of the village's unpaid-for social services. After all, why make a fruitless call which would cost you money when the information was freely available. Information — you

20

may call it gossip if you like — is an essential trading commodity in a village.

I do not recall ever hearing the word "alcoholic" until I was at least twenty years old. We did not have alcoholics in our village. We had more than our share of the county's drunkards, and like the telephone operator, we watched over them. My great uncle Rainbow was not given that name for following a drab way of life.

We then lived in a world in which there were no finger-wagging agents of the Nanny State telling the village drunkards about brain damage caused by loss of logic capacities, oxygenation of the blood, of the creeping death of the non-regenerating liver. The village watched over Rainbow and his wastrel friends and guided their footsteps, when absolutely necessary, to their various tiny cottages. (They said that "the drink" would get Rainbow in the end. It did. He died at ninety-four with a countryman's indifference as to which direction he might next travel.)

A visit from the district nurse — heavily moustached, and who I imagined to have been born at the age of fifty and had remained at that age all her life, puffing and wheezing like an asthmatic badger — was a combination of scandal sheet, newspaper and the wireless. She was paid to participate in everyone's life from the cradle to the grave. Lurid stories of difficult childbirth enthralled the middle-aged ladies of the village and made me wonder why apparently unintelligent sheep could manage so easily, while supposedly intelligent humans made such a fuss about a simple function of nature.

Like little pigs with big ears we hung on her every word . . . and often ended up having to be comforted in the night for the nightmares they brought on.

For commercial reasons I had to live part of the working week in a leafy London suburb overlooking a royal park. My neighbour, who lived in this street for forty years prided himself that he did not know all the other residents by name — there are only twenty-six houses in the street — and that he had never spoken to some of the families even though they had lived there as long as he had. What a terrible loss.

Then the summer ripens and the columns of weekend cars trundle out of the cities, some to weekend at a country cottage, some to holiday for the odd week before they can get to the Mediterranean sun, and I began to realise that the attitude of urban insularity was being insidiously exported from town to country.

Cars numbered by the thousand hurtle down the Birmingham/Taunton motorway. The people in the motorway cars seem to believe in increasing numbers that because they have brief access to the country they have a right to say how it will be managed. But not from the countryside they visit — but from the urban centres where all the big decisions are made.

Take another point: a distant Prime Minister removed tax relief from second homes. The idea was to penalise the rich. But the rich continued to buy their country cottages simply because they are rich, and those who did sell them did so at prices based on city values and the village continued to exclude its poor. That Prime

Minister had forgotten that all men are born equal . . . but different.

I stood in the middle of a Huntingdon field with a sporting Earl — he left over £10,000,000 when he died. He was swopping information, as an equal, with a group of didicais. Information — poking your nose — is vital in the country. The source is not always important. Gossip has a currency value of its own.

But into the country cottage condition, where the gap between town and country is measurably widening, despite the continued existence of various government sponsored commissions, come the town-folk. They come, they appear to see very little and they do not participate.

Certainly they patronise the village shop, and I use the word in the less pleasant sense, and they like to have a pint in the local with the village "characters" . . . it is fun to "slum it" in the public bar rather than the carpeted "lounge". But would they guide the latter day Rainbow home? I doubt it. They are also offended if you want to know too much about their private lives. It is not that we really want to know if that silver-haired man is married to that young woman. Our curiosity may be based on envy, or vicarious living or, more probably, trying to fit them into their proper place in village life. We are only poking our noses.

In the countryside a village jumble sale is not a means of redistributing local wealth. It is an informal parliament where often fiercely conflicting views are traded and important local issues aligned. The weekenders do not attend jumble sales. They do not want three size seventeen collarless shirts marked with the wartime economy label and I did not want a badly worn, plated asparagus dish. But it was a small price I paid for learning that twenty-two red hinds were resting up on Miss Collins's pasture. And note that precision; not a herd, but twenty-two specific red hinds.

The village shop is also not patronised by the weekenders, they bring much more sophisticated food with them together with endless bottles of wine and curious coloured spirits. But it is not simply a place where you leave your keys for the friends who will be using your cottage next weekend. You should also leave your most personal and intimate secrets there, secure in the knowledge that everyone in the parish will know them by morning.

Then a new vicar arrived, an Oxford graduate with four children at public schools. We were all deeply impressed and knew in an instant he would never get on. In the country the rich and the poor have a deep affinity because they know who they are; they do not have problems of identity. It is the socially aspiring and the weekenders who irritate because they take refuge in secrecy and fail to know that they have too little of consequence to hide. Hiding requires isolation and an emotional drawbridge which keeps them locked in but does not necessarily keep us out.

The vicar's wife took a large box to the home, well, it was more a shanty than a home, of Willie Richards, an elderly gardener. (Why is it that gardeners never retire but work right on to the end of their days?)

"It is to put your clothes in," the vicar's wife said.

"And me sit on top of it all naked and cold?" he replied.

If only she had asked. It is not that we ever poked our noses into Willie's private life, he kept himself to himself and appeared to live in a world of permanent humorous imagination as he was often seen smiling to himself at some private joke. But it was the most natural thing in our world to know that he was the sort of man who needed life to provide him with just one suit.

Participation in village life is not always organising the local ecology protection group and the village preservation society to clean out the pond, remove the bikes and the bedsteads. It may be just in getting closer to your neighbour even if you can smell Willie's suit in the next parish. Incidentally, that box is still empty, I know it without crossing the threshold . . . or poking my nose. But Willie does find it useful to have his dinner on.

Then came the winter. Cattle were brought into covered yards to prevent them cutting up the meadows and help keep them clean for milking. They stand about as if waiting for something to happen, knowing that nothing will ever happen.

But the bullocks were left out in the rain-swept fields, and more for exercise than work the Shire was harnessed up and a light load of silage or hay was loaded. Drake — whoever would call an 18.2hh Shire "Drake"? — hated the rain-filled ruts in farm gates and had to be trotted through, the farmer holding the head bridle. As they approached the deep mud he swung his feet off the ground and was whirled over the morass.

25

And then came Christmas. Would you, if I asked, look at Christmas from a different point of view? There were 80 guernseys to be milked. That meant getting up at four in the morning. There is no fun milking cows with a hangover, so Christmas Eve was, and is, celebrated modestly. It also meant going back at three in the afternoon. It did not give much time to sip port and gaze at the logs blazing on the fire. Also the horses had to be fed and groomed. The goat would, no doubt, be having another phantom pregnancy and be behaving in a mawkish fashion.

Animals demand attention 365 days a year; they do not take days out of life, and Christmas is as much another day to them as Midsummer day. Whatever day it is, they are always waiting for nothing to happen.

Up in Bishopsdale people take Christmas seriously. As autumn creeps slowly down the dale they start to buy in their flour and sugar and other essential foods by the sack and by the case. One Christmas when it snowed, my friends did not see a neighbour for nine days. They are only eleven miles from the nearest shop in Leyburn, so what are a few days this or that side of Christmas?

It isn't that country people "manage" or "cope" with winter; they take for granted that it will be cold, that there will be snow and in north Yorkshire and the Cleveland hills they will be digging out the clusters of ewes from under the drifts. Someone once said, "Too long a winter" but I rather think he has never wintered above Richmond where austerity is not a way of life, it is life.

26

However, I find that it is that lovable, naive, tragic Victorian, Reverend Francis Kilvert in Radnorshire, who puts Christmas on my map with a stamp of iron:

"As I lay awake praying in the early morning I thought I heard a sound of distant bells. It was an intense frost. I sat down in my bath on a sheet of thick ice, which broke in the middle into large pieces whilst sharp points and jagged edges stuck all round the sides like *chevaux de frise*, not particularly comforting to the naked thighs and loins, for the keen ice was like broken glass. The ice water stung and scorched like fire. I had to collect the floating pieces of ice and pile them on a chair before I could use the sponge and then I had to thaw the sponge for it was a mass of ice. The morning was most brilliant!"

There is no doubt that as a clergyman he was familiar with my old pal, Job, the biblical farmer who wrote: "By the breath of God frost is given . . ."

But how did we come to lose Francis Kilvert's sense of wonder and innocence of Christmas? There was a story he heard, and he was sure the old woman who told it to him was pulling his leg, about the animals in the byre, kneeling towards Bethlehem in homage at midnight on Christmas Eve. But the story is still told in the country, I think because many people want to believe it.

Not, of course, that there is a shortage of references to animals in the Bible. Not just the fabled ox and the ass of the nativity stable or the possibly unceremonious Palm Sunday donkey.

The dog gets something like 150 mentions, most of which the contemporary public relations man would call a "bad press", largely because the dog does in public what the human does in private. But there are plenty of references to the lion which possibly existed in Israel into this century, to the eagle, perhaps even to the hippo — although he is not referred to by name — and even to one mythical beast, the unicorn — could this be the sad-faced oryx — but wait until you hear the eulogy for the horse.

Job, the farmer, who wrote about animals with an excitement bordering on ecstasy — he had over 10,000 sheep by the way — said: "Hast thou given the horse strength? Hast thou clothed his neck with thunder? Canst thou make him afraid as a grasshopper? The glory of his nostrils is terrible . . . he rejoiceth in his strength . . . he mocketh at fear . . ."

Nothing has changed down here since Job herded his sheep and put pen to paper.

But the thing which puzzles me about the Bible is that there is, as far as I can see, no mention of the cat. Surely, if cats were worshipped as gods and adored as pets in next door Egypt, they must have been known in ancient Palestine.

Were they even then,

> No less liquid than their shadows, offering no
>   angles to the wind . . .
> They slip, diminished, neat, through loopholes
> Less than themselves.

Where they always there but never seen?

But the moment I mention animals in the Bible, and if wrongly at that, my friends point out the error of my ways. One said: "The Bible is indeed a book of beasts from the first page onwards but there are no cats there at all." Strangely they are mentioned in the Roman Catholic Bible, in the book of Baruch in the so-called Epistle of Jeremy which is also included in that very strange book, the Apocrypha and this Master Jeremy also appears in the Orthodox Church so that the great majority of Christians do have reference to cats in their scriptures.

This started me off, with the help of a friend, on some detective work on animals and I was amazed to find that the Christmas story of the ox and the ass — whether kneeling towards Bethlehem or not — are not mentioned in the New Testament at all! The first reference is amongst the fulsome writings, or should it be rantings, of Isaiah, "The ox knoweth his owner and the ass his master's crib".

I am told that the earliest artistic representation of the Nativity animals is on a fourth-century marble sarcophagus in the Lateran Museum in Rome where the ox and the ass warm the child with their breath. But what thrilled me most of all was to discover that St Francis of Assisi — the man who talked to the birds and the animals and is close to the hearts of all those who love animals — originated the practice of placing a crib in church at Greccio in 1223, in which the ox and the ass had an essential place. It is said that Christmas carols grew out of this innovation and this is the reason why they are so often mentioned.

It is not for people like myself to take on the book of Genesis: "Let us make man in our image, and let them have dominion over the fish of the sea, and over the fowl of the air and over the cattle . . ." I think I might prefer to live with them as equals.

Stand at the stable door on Christmas night and listen to the quiet harmony of horses at peace and you will easily believe even these giants knelt towards Bethlehem, and you hope they will inspire you to be big enough to have your own neck "clothed in thunder".

But there is another aspect of Christmas which dies hard in the country and that is the telling of the traditional ghost story. Some are like the tale of the man picked at the roadside and placed on the roof of a coach and lent a greatcoat because he is shivering with cold in the torrential rain. When the coach arrives at the inn the man hurries inside and the coat is found hanging on the back of a chair . . . perfectly dry. The opposite occurs the next day when it is dry and the coat is found to be sopping wet.

After many questions it is found that he was murdered at the spot where the coach finds him, but many years ago and he is not shivering with cold . . . but trembling with fear.

I have heard this story in various forms from Hampshire to Inverness and everyone who told it to me swears it is true and that is why that piece of road is called "Dead Man's Hill".

May I ask you also to look at ghosts from a different point of view: my uncle and my uncle's ghosts — don't be alarmed, there are only two of them — are in conflict over the morning newspaper. His ghosts appear every day, in the bright heat of a summer day, when the mist hangs like the thin silver hair of an old woman on the marshes or in the chill of winter.

But the momemt you start talking about anything which exists within the quotation marks "supernatural" you are sure to be dismissed as a crank. But when sane, rational, men fully at home with all the modern sciences have regular and continuous experience of extra-material presences then you should think again.

Our thoughts are muddied by the exaggerations when tales are told in front of the pub fire and they are masked by the idea that ghosts are not only frightening but malevolent. Talking to people with uninvited guests, they seem to be more plentiful in the country than the great cities where you may hear of a malicious poltergeist. I am convinced that most ghosts are warm and friendly and to my uncle's certain knowledge, at worst only a nuisance.

You have to learn to live with your ghost.

My first experience with ghosts was, forgive the pun, extraordinary. I was standing in the hallway looking up the stairs of our spacious Victorian (built 1850) family house on a hot summer Saturday and saw two small ladies in black on the mezzanine. I walked a mile up the hill to the pub before it dawned on me that I could not possibily have seen what I thought I had seen. But I *had* left the front door open as they were obviously going out.

It was still open when I got back and my wife said that I was talking cider-inspired rubbish, but the eldest daughter (then the only daughter and hardly more than a tousle-head) remarked chirpily, "Oh yes, those two old ladies who live in the middle bedroom . . ."

I put the thought of ghosts out of mind — they were the only ones I have ever seen — until many years later. Then a friend who lives on the edge of a small town in Surrey took me to one side and said that while he was working on some meticulous drawings he noticed a man in a grey suit in his studio. He was a little surprised at not hearing him come up the stairs to the studio which is filled with every piece of electronic wizardry any designer could wish for.

His wife, a woman so profoundly uncomplicated that I am surprised she does not take root in the ground, asked him who his friend was as she had not heard the front door open and close, although he had popped his head round the kitchen door where she was stirring Monday's lunch-time skillet.

The man returned each day and the same routine took place until their son came into the house to complain that a man in a neat grey suit had come into the garden and, uninvited, had prodded at his bonfire with a stick. Now, small boys get possessive about their bonfires. It was, of course, the same man in each case, but my friend feared that if he told his wife what he believed to be the truth she would desert the house forever.

Never under-estimate the intuition or courage of a woman with an uninvited guest. She had twigged on his second visit. The well-dressed man pops into Angie's kitchen most days and they are getting on well together. She does the talking, he is always silent. The son told him to clear off from the garden, which he politely did, but he still goes up to the studio most days to supervise the work in progress.

Not so with my uncle's ghost. This resident insists on smoking his pipe in the upstairs loo and frequently popping into the closest and flushing the ancient plumbing system so that all the pipes gurgle and burp round the house. This is not imagination, almost everyone who visits the house sees him, hears him and smells the ghost's foul pipe, sees the water swirling in the pan, hears the plumbing bleating like a herd of ewes.

Even when my uncle bought the mill house it was derelict ... but cheap ... and always reputed to have been haunted. And as so often happens with ghosts there is a residual sadness about them. Going back through the county archives and the files of the country newspaper he was able to find, in every tragic detail, the story of the rich miller and the drowning of his daughter in the mill dam where the two great water wheels have now stopped thundering, beside the quay where the wherries and the spritsail barges, crewed by the traditional "one man, a boy and a dog", carried away the flour and meal no longer tie up.

What irritates my uncle and puzzles all of us is that the miller comes into the morning room when he is reading the *Daily Telegraph* and peers over his shoulder, resting his elbow on him. If you should turn the page before the miller has finished reading it he turns it back.

My cousin became annoyed that the ghost of the little drowned girl kept throwing his daughter's toys around the playroom and taking them from her cot. So he sat and waited for the ghost of the child and tried to pick her up . . . but you can't, can you? But if you can't, why can you feel the pressure of the miller's arm on your shoulder — he also tends to shove you, with force, out of the way if you are rummaging in the fridge for something to eat.

But the miller's time sequence seems to have a double loop: the ghost appears every day through a built-in wardrobe in a bedroom. After years of research — in the days when this house was built you simply built your house in the style and size you wanted, there were no architect's plans and no fussy "town planners" — it was discovered that there had once been a back staircase which led into that room.

But if the miller, who died 127 years ago, can only find a now non-existent staircase why will he be in the morning room reading today's news?

He should remember that mature men feel about their newspapers what small boys feel about their bonfires.

But learning to live with your ghost took a new twist the other day. My uncle was in his kitchen — it is rather larger than the average kitchen — making a pot of tea for a friend. The kettle was boiled, the tea pot warmed, the tea carefully measured and left to draw.

The miller, who was in his customary position, leaning on his beloved fridge, watched these laborious proceedings in his usual silence as my uncle poured three cups of tea. "Why", the friend asked, "are you pouring three cups of tea?"

"Oh," my uncle said vaguely. "I thought the miller might like one . . ."

CHAPTER
THREE

The Smallest Child

Animals fascinate me. They also puzzle me endlessly and sometimes infuriate me beyond endurance. I say this because a donkey came to stay. She was uninvited, of course, as are so many of our guests.

Her owner was one of those amiable misfits you find in villages. He had been an architect of sorts, designing farm buildings . . . of a very curious sort, the sort that appeared on paper to be wholly adequate, until you came to build them when you discovered that the doors could not be put where they should be, the windows were never square and the roofs rarely survived the first puff of a winter gale.

He became a firewood merchant, often finding logs before they were lost, and wandered around the village with his donkey and cart until he was taken ill in the high street. The donkey and cart were brought to our yard, where, unable to see over the stable door, the donkey stood in silent misery staring at the rubble wall.

Until morning, that is, when her dawn chorus could be heard in the next county. She was quickly released into the paddocks, temporarily on loan to a rag-tag and bobtail of indifferent hacks from a riding stable. She eyed these horses with deep caution and kept well out of their way.

Walking the dogs in the morning fields the next day the donkey came up to me in what I thought was either only curiosity or friendship. But she suddenly spun round and, with hooves sharp as arrows, lashed out. I thought the floppy-eared devil had broken my leg as I writhed in the dewy grass. Later that day I heard that the moke's owner had died. Was she already, by that strange telepathy common to horses and donkeys, aware of his death? Was she angry or upset and taking it out on me?

I offered the donkey back to the widow as it is not uncommon for men down here to make their last journey in their own traps. "No thank you," the widow said. Although generously intended the gift to me was about as welcome as a visitation of foot and mouth disease.

The next day, by necessity, I carried a stout ash walking stick. The donkey came over to have a look at me, but as she spun round to kick she got a whack on her quarters. She looked at me, frowning and tried to kick again only to get another crisp whack.

But the following morning, having been awakened by the unorchestrated braying of Peggy, as we had now discovered her name to be, an even more unusual and unexplainable act of animal behaviour took place. We were only half way through the first field when the donkey came up, eager to mug me, but as she squared up for the kick and I grasped my stick defensively, one of the riding stable mares came over at a brisk trot, her head held high and unusually lifting her fore-ends like a Hackney horse.

In a moment she had pushed herself, head to tail, between Peggy and myself. The donkey skeltered round to find clear ground for her morning attack but the mare consistently put herself between Peggy and my stick, and as we walked up the fields to the lookout the mare maintained her buffer role despite all the donkey's angry cavorting.

And so this ritual went on for several days. The donkey tried every cunning ruse; she would walk away as if disinterested and then try to gallop back when she thought the mare was not looking but she was always thwarted, the mare sometimes coming between us so quickly and closely that I was almost knocked off my feet.

Two things puzzled me: the other horses in those fields appeared to take no notice at all of the self-appointed role of the mare. They continued to graze undisturbed. The point was that the donkey entirely ignored the dogs; many horses would attack and chase them, while many others, I agree, would not. I appeared, for reasons I shall never know, the sole focus of her antagonism, but after a week Peggy's odd behaviour changed again and I detected the change in an instant. She walked slowly over to us and the mare, her head down, grazing, ignored her. A moment later a quaint procession was strolling up the fields . . . one man, canine old age pensioners, rioting pups, distinguished matrons from the greyhound kennels and one donkey in line astern.

Peggy now decided she would rather be a dog. She would not be left in the fields. She insisted on following the procession home; came into the kitchen where she peered about with unconcealed curiosity, ate her rations in a dog pen and followed me about in the garden. As the goat habitually followed me about as well, looking at me with her wicked yellow eyes, I had plenty of company.

The donkey was put to work in her little cart and started showing extraordinary affection, pushing her head under my arm like a headless ghost if I stood about with my hands in my pockets.

It was all too good to last. One afternoon, as we toiled together in the potato plot, she stopped. Nothing would budge her. She would not move, did not mutter a single word, but no persuasion, no temptations would shift her.

She was released from harness and then, only slowly, would she be led to the stable. The vet greeted Peggy with a great shout of recognition. She is tired out, he claimed, "So would you be if you were as old as she is". The vet had known her for over twenty years and she was no girl when they had first met. She was now closer to thirty than twenty years old.

We were advised to let nature take its course. But a few mornings later we knew she had died, simply slipped away in the night and left us to a silent morning.

She lay in the straw as if in gentle sleep and for all her bad temper, her eccentricities and her disloyalty I grieved for her. Through her the veil of darkness between man and donkey and man and horse had, if only briefly, been raised and I had been lucky enough to be there when the light shone.

Then the smallest child came stomping into the kitchen in her muddy wellies and announced to an astonished world that a cat was making a nest in the herb garden and was about to lay an egg. We take such opinions seriously. An expedition was hastily mounted. There was the cat, inelegantly seated in a clump of wild thyme, with a big fat grin all over his face. There was no egg.

The cat was carried by the smallest child back to the house to be told the facts of life. This incident set me thinking about the way we touch animals and that we do not consciously appreciate the importance they play in our lives. There are, of course, some people who do not like animals at all. I believe they are the poorer for it.

From their earliest days we urged the children to touch animals; the boar pig rests his elbows on the sty wall and watches our futile labours with small, sad eyes. He is waiting for a treat of carrots and apples. A huge onion makes his tummy rumble like an orchestra tuning up. But his wife farrowed twelve piglets as pink and small as human children. We put our children into the sty while the shoots were asleep under the straw. The result was chaos, laughter and falls, some cuddles for the little pigs and a stern rebuff from the sow.

We also put our children into Harold Huff's lambing pen to show them the facts of life. Lambs were coming out of ewes like corks out of pop-guns. The smallest child, crouching and watching this simple and beautiful act of life, wondered why lambs have to be licked clean.

"Don't their mummies have tissues?" the smallest child asked.

But there is a much more serious side to our antics. It is widely accepted that animals can play an important role in psycho-therapy. There are many mentally damaged people who will accept the love and affection of a dog or cat before they can give or accept love from a human. There are many documented cases where people have been brought out of hospitals through contact with animals; one, a woman who had spent thirty years in various institutions.

Even the simple touch of a dog to a person who has had a heart attack reduces the stress in that human and helps to cure his ills. So what then can the cuddling of an ugly muffin of a tabby cat mean to lonely people?

Setters are craftily used at Great Barr where mentally handicapped children are described with kindness and deep love as "at the bottom of the barrel" of humanity.

But we can open the barrel and the horse is the key: Henry Blake, the tetraplegic author on the psychology of horses, can bring his horses down from the hill by thought transference and Joe Royds, who lives above the river at Glasbury on Wye, has discovered there is a form of non-verbal communication between mentally handicapped children and horses.

Scientists laugh at such ideas but we know because we have seen it happen so often, time after time and day after day, that it cannot be accident or coincidence, so we believe it must be true even though those scientists call it only "anecdotal evidence". Here then is an anecdote: Joe had a mare with the temperament of Attila

41

the Hun. She bit everyone, kicked indescriminantly and was so badly behaved that, even though her tail was red-ribboned as a warning to all, she was sent home from the hunt.

But a small mentally handicapped boy used her tail to climb aboard; he stood beneath her and pulled handfuls of hair from her udders . . . and she stood there with a benign smile on her face. So the mare was loaded up and taken to a local special school to give the children rides and where she was as good as gold. From this it was concluded that she would tolerate the severely handicapped entirely, the less handicapped occasionally, and very young normal children but unhandicapped adults never. What was uncanny was her ability to distinguish the difference on sight and at a distance.

Over the years and having put up many thousands of handicapped children we discovered that thoroughbred horses communicate in the non-verbal sense more quickly than non-blood horses and the communication works best with horses and ponies, well-bred donkeys and in one isolated but recorded case, would you believe it, with a Somali racing camel. But, again, that is a thoroughbred animal.

A friend who had been a district commissioner in northern Kenya told me that it is common in the Arab world for mentally handicapped people to be camel minders. In village life in Britain in previous centuries the "village idiot" was most often employed with the great horses that populated our farms and they even became proficient at rudimentary veterinary techniques.

I think that the great horse and the village idiot understood each other even though they could not converse, and surely it was better to employ people in the community than to tuck them away, out of sight, out of mind, in a grim and unloving institution.

Evidence of this communication without speech, which certainly hardly ever occurs with normal people, is that when the handicapped child mounts the horse there is a sudden and visible change in the horse's alertness, a change in the position of the ears and frequently a juggling change of pace. But Welsh cobs and ponies and cobs usually "bridle", drop their chins towards their chests; Fell ponies shorten their stride without altering the position of their head.

In the human there is an equal change in behaviour; a screaming, kicking child either instantly or certainly after only thirty to fifty seconds relaxes and usually throws himself forward for the apparent direct, sensual contact with the horse.

Frequently the mounted autistic child can be helped. Joe knows of twenty-seven recorded cases where mute children, often autists, have spoken from the saddle, will make chortling noises as if singing and will peer about at the world, seeing it from a different viewpoint, that of the arrogant horseman who looks down upon his inferiors.

The sceptics will be asking how we can tell that thoroughbreds are best in this therapy: a boy was riding in a school playground and was showing all the signs of being in non-verbal touch with the horse when the horse came to a fence beyond which were some tatty-headed, flop-eared donkeys inquisitively attracted to the day's events by the many voices.

Face to face with these Jacks and Jennies, the horse showed all the characteristics of going out of communication ... and the child followed suit. The child stopped singing, the horse slumped to a casual walk. Turning the horse's back on the donkeys the communication immediately returned. This was tried several times and, uncannily, it happened every time.

So an independent experiment had to be conducted between a pony and a mixture of donkeys. Face to face it was found that communication did not lapse with the known-to-be better bred donkeys, but lapsed immediately with the introduction of a moke.

Then things took a bizzare turn: Henry Blake is convinced that there is a high degree of telepathy between horses, possibly between all herd animals and packs of dogs whether wild or domestic, so why should we be surprised if telepathy occurs in uncontaminated human minds such as the Australian Aborigines, Bushmen, Esquimaux ... why then should it not occur in the uncontaminated minds of mentally handicapped children?

The bizzare event was this: Joe had two horses and had taken the kicker and biter away in a trailer horse box. On the way home he had a puncture and stopped to change the wheel. A friend, who takes care of his animals when he is away, was feeding and watering the companion horse which was grazing placidly.

Suddenly its behaviour became oddly erratic, even distressed. It dunged and scuffed the dung about. By chance the friend glanced at his watch and the next day recounted the experience to Joe. The time was exactly that when the puncture occurred and the erratic behaviour lasted as long as it took to change the wheel because Joe looked at his watch to see how much time he had lost in the repairs.

I ask the simple question: did the companion horse know her friend was in distress? I cannot believe it was coincidence. But shortly afterwards there was an opportunity to check this behaviour in a slightly more scientific way. The kicker and biter went down a steep bank and crashed into a brook and could not get out. It was a block and tackle job with a Land-Rover to rescue this equine nuisance, but she was injured. The friend was asked to take care of the animals and Joe boxed her up and drove into Brecon to the vet for attention to the mare's gashed belly. They checked their watches.

The agitated and erratic behaviour happened again — except for those minutes when the mare was anaesthetised. (There is a lot of difference to the brain between being asleep and being unconscious and horses, incidentally, sleep properly for only two hours a day.) Quite simply, the companion horse had lost telepathic communication with its friend. At the exact second the mare's eyelids started to flicker, returning to consciousness from the anaesthetic, the behaviour of the companion horse changed again and she settled down and returned to her normal placid life. Did she know her friend was again safe?

Of course, this is only anecdotal evidence. But there is many an unlettered countryman who has watched his animals over the years with both care and love and with that deep personal knowledge of each individual that I would trust before I put my faith in scientists. So I am not surprised that a mentally handicapped child can rush into the box of a thoroughbred stallion and roll in the straw beneath his feet while the horse, known to have a savage temper and to be only just this side of being unmanageable, continues to eat as if undisturbed — or that the kicker and biter should allow children to play in-and-out-the-windows between her legs.

Deep in thought about animals and the fact that I, too, have lost this basic communication with animals through the contamination of urbanisation, I walked my dogs up the hill. There was a Guernsey in labour and in distress. The farmer, a short man with shoulders as broad as a bus, was struggling on the ground to turn the head of the calf which would not eject from the cow. He has fists like iron and is more likely to punch you in the face than say "Good Morning". They make farmers hard down here.

He toiled for an hour before the calf died and the vet arrived. Then he turned away from me, tears streaming down his whiskery face. The bobby calf was not worth a pound of anyone's money. Hardly worth fifty pence. But we had lost an animal. And that hurts, especially when you know the true value of animals.

But there is no end to the mysteries of animal behaviour: a tall wind stalked the downs. To the west of us Warminster; and lost in the folds of the downs, Chitterne, where Samuel Pepys is reputed to have stayed while on his travels. But precisely where we were I shall never know.

We were homeward bound after a week of watching racehorses on the gallops in the dawn, stamping our feet and blowing on our fingers until that unearthly and inexpressibly beautiful sight of galloping racehorses emerged out of the mist, mobile and fluid Grecian statues, and thundered past only to be swallowed up in the mist again. Then, to the jumps to see young, fearless men put a thousand pounds weight of horse over a jump almost five feet high at thirty miles an hour.

Now a new sun shone on the cold and we watched, from those heights, the distant discomfort of foxhunters. It was like looking down on them from the eyes of a kestrel over a tussocky field. The Master and Huntsman were heading in one direction unsighted by the field which was heading away from them, while "the sandy whiskered gentleman" strolled slowly down the fence about fifty yards from us. Was he the one Solomon had in mind when he wrote:

> Take us the foxes, the little foxes,
> That spoil the vine.

He had spoiled no vines, but he had spoiled the hunt, at least for the time being.

The children and I struggled down a steep bank — the smallest child had to be carried — and the fox looked up, his face showing no alarm, no curiosity. As we approached he set off at a walk up a gentle slope of stubbles.

We trudged behind and if we walked faster, he walked faster: if we stopped, he stopped and turned and looked at us; if we ran, he ran; but whatever we did he maintained fifty yards distance. Following foxhounds on foot — I need to see what happens in my country before I make up my mind whether I am for or agin' it — I noted exactly the same pattern. Eventually our "Gentleman" crept into a vast island of brambles and gorse, no doubt carefully created as a fox covert, where he sat some six feet in, peering at us without fear or curiosity. He seemed to know that we would tire of the game first.

Explaining this experience to a young man in another county; the sort of young man who wears a gaberdine mac in high summer, leather boots but no socks; he said that in looking at birds and animals every observation is different. You may, he said, see animal behaviour which is truly unique, not just for that species but unique to that animal for a first and only time.

I thought about this when the vixen, "our vixen", a skinny creature with a narrow mask, which comes from an earth the size of a diamond mine in the railway embankment, crosses a garden, a road and a second garden before quartering my lawns for worms and insects. You would be surprised at the variety of food a fox will eat.

In winter she pawed the snow away to eat the covered birdseed, oblivious of the watchers in the night. But recently she has come to the sliding windows of a brightly lit room and, like a cat playing soft-paw or sitting in my kitchen sink trying to catch silver jewels as they drip from the tap, she touches the glass, looks puzzled, moves on and reaches out for the glass, still puzzled, before resuming her nightly wanderings. The smallest child looks up from her book or from the ubiquitous television screen and makes no comment about the vixen. She has become part of the family.

A quarter of a mile away another vixen brings her cubs into a spacious lawn as if some unseen bosun had piped, "All hands to the foredeck for dancing and skylarking". The games they play are rough, noisy and boisterous.

Only a further quarter mile away, in the spooky dereliction of the grounds of what had once been a grand Georgian house (although it has long since gone, you can still feel it brooding between the majestic blue cedars, its dead eyes gazing out on a departed world) the vixen strolls to within a few feet of the eight foot wall, suddenly accelerates and runs up the wall with the dexterity of a fleeing spider. Then she drops onto the compost heap on the other side where she scavenges for her cubs and where she also picks up all sorts of exotic titbits simply because the lady of the house feeds her. Quite why I do not know. Foxes are natural survivors and I believe that even after the ultimate nuclear holocaust the foxes will still be here smiling at the world and getting on with their business.

But then, one balmy night, when it appeared that someone had polished the moon for the personal benefit of the writers of sentimental songs, I was walking with my Basset hound down a narrow path between oceans of bracken, when I heard a deep voice barking.

Instinctively I stopped to assess distance and direction. It was a huge dog fox, but so profound a baritone it might easily have been mistaken at first for a domestic dog except that it had that harsh edge to its voice which says "fox" amongst all the other night sounds on the heath. I walked slowly forward on the springy turf, cut low by generations of rabbits until I could see into the clearing in the bracken.

A vixen and her three cubs were sitting on their haunches in a rough line. The huge dog fox walked slowly away from them until he was some thirty yards distant . . . then he turned, and barking furiously as he gained speed he raced towards the vixen and cubs.

When only a few feet from them he rolled over and over across the grass several times. He got up, shook himself and repeated the game, to the apparent indifference of the vixen and the cubs who watched without showing any appreciation. And he did this five times before I silently crept away.

I had seen something unique, truly unique, both to the species and to that animal. Even the Department of Zoology at Oxford University, where they have forgotten more about fox behaviour than I have ever learned, had not heard of such odd behaviour.

Around here they say: "The fox knows everything — the hedgehog knows one big thing." I think I shall give up fox watching. It is becoming uncanny and perhaps the gentle hedgehog knows the answer to the fox's antics.

But then, of course, I could always ask the smallest child . . .

CHAPTER
FOUR

High Life

I have an uneasy feeling that the gap between the country and the town is widening and I believe this is because of, not despite, the series of beautifully filmed, intelligently scripted and meticulously researched television programmes broadcast at peak-viewing times, and the many wildlife programmes sent singing through the air on the wireless.

Let me explain: periodically I would walk my ancient Basset hound at night with my neighbour and his pair of Labrador bitches. He often sat in his huge Victorian house during the evenings watching wildlife programmes and during our strolls I would get detailed reports of the implantation of ovaries in seals. Or I might get an erudite résumé on the Wandering Albatross or the bizarre neglect of the Browed Albatross and its solitary chick in the fierce cold of the Antarctic ice-cap ... Manatees in the swamp rivers of Florida, and the symbiotic relationship between the sloth and its passenger moths and the lichens which grow on its coat.

As we were walking a vixen hopped over a garden wall almost as if she were a shadow of herself and trotted down the pavement with that fluid movement unhurried foxes own. My neighbour took no notice, made no comment. Then I realised why . . . he thought it was a dog. But he had seen Stephen Harris's programmes about urban foxes and David MacDonald's nightview of Oxford foxes and their territories. But what he had seen was out of context: the vixen on that pavement would have been fascinating — if she had been on television. My neighbour would have talked about her with all the authority that he recently talked about vast rookeries of Hopper penguins and of Blue Whales singing in the Atlantic deeps.

What television and, to a lesser extent, wireless has done is to provide information without education and knowledge without participation. I have a dismal view that for all the television in the world my neighbour would not spot a fox's earth or be able to tell which of a colony of badger setts is currently occupied. He has never smelt the rancid stench of a red stag's rutting pit and yet, behind the tall wall under which we were walking, there were a dozen or more rutting pits.

It is as if there is an imaginary line drawn across people's minds that "The Countryside" ends at a specific point on a city's perimeter and "The City" starts the other side of that line.

Nothing could be further from the truth and there are two anecdotes which illustrate my point about observation and participation in urban wildlife: a friend met the late Laureate, John Betjeman, leaving the vast and heavily populated Royal Automobile Club after dinner ("Being a member of the RAC is rather like being a member of Paddington station", he once remarked) and they walked together through the deserted midnight streets of London, Sir John busily pointing out all the little architectural trills and fancies which, to him, gave character or fantasy to buildings. He said that people walked about with their eyes at eye level, they never looked upwards.

For three years, while I owned a house in Teddington, I kept a fox watch in the deserted grounds where once, according to the faded photographs in the local history book, had stood a that grand Georgian mansion. The cedars were still there and the pines for the breeze to whisper in, and even a deep sense of foreboding that the dead eyes of the windows of the mansion were looking at this plebian intruder. In one corner stood a box-like police station of negative architectural merit. The remainder was surrounded with a wall twelve feet high at the front, and eight feet high at the sides and all this less than 200 yards from the busiest shopping street in the town.

Yet no-one except the one lady who fed the vixen while the cubs were still underground seemed to be aware that they existed. One year she had three cubs and in the two following years, four. She marked out her territory and, having found an easy way at the back to climb over the wall I would drop down into the undergrowth at dawn and dusk to collect her garbage and analyse her scavengings.

To say that a fox is omnivorous is to throw away a good joke to an unhearing audience. "My" vixen, or should I say "The Inspector's" vixen, lived high on the hog, mainly from dustbin raids.

"Whoever did that," my fireside naturalist friend said, surveying his capsized dustbins and their scattered contents, "ought to be shot." It was, of course, the vixen that I had seen the previous night and he had not, and if he had complained to the police about vandalism the inspector would have been more than embarrassed — it's his vixen.

Then there are the rich pickings from the remains of take-away chicken dinners thrown into the town's gutters; bones and meat scraps neatly tied into old prepacked bread bags and equally neatly torn open by the vixen. That says nothing about the baked bean cans licked clean and strewn around the mouth of the earth. But when I came to analyse fox droppings, (they are like smell-less thick dark baize and do not disintegrate easily as they are solidified with the fur of their prey), I found in town all the usual foods of the country fox, identified by their bones and particularly their jaws and teeth: the bones of field mice and bank voles, the hard wing cases of beetles and blackberry pips, haw-berries and perhaps — I am not sure — seeds of the poisonous Woody Nightshade (*Solanum dulcamara*).

Dr Harris in Bristol found the remains of a Chinese take-away dinner and an ice lolly stick in the stomachs of road casualty foxes. And in this I have discovered a possible paradox between urban and country foxes. It is a statement as yet unproven: that road casualties are less, by a wide margin, in towns than in country areas near motorways and main roads because urban drivers are more alert to the sudden appearance of dogs, small children, even adults, from behind parked cars. But it does work the other way round: returning from a reception late one night a grey fox crossed the road almost under our wheels in Twickenham and our excitement was so great that *we* almost crashed our own car.

By the time I had marked out all the earths I could find, reports were coming in that foxes were scavenging restaurant detritus left out overnight in Cannon Street in the heart of the City of London and that the scavengers were coming down from Highgate and Enfield, at least ten miles distant, for the pleasure.

The questions of course are "why" and "how"? The fact that over 200 species of wild birds are recorded in Greater London and the number of swallows, martins and swifts has increased are coincidental to the various Clean Air acts. But there are other reasons:

> My men, like satyrs grazing on the lawn
> Shall with their goat feet dance the antic hay

said Andrew Marvell in his mysterious couplet. Was he alluding to the present day green and silver tunnels which lure the country into town so that a startled motorist encounters a roe deer dancing its "antic hay" in Putney High Street? The particular green tunnel which lured this animal into urban life starts at Esher and leads gently though Weston Green to the Home Park at Hampton Court Palace, the thousand acres of Bushey Park, so under-used in the week that foxes bask in the sunshine outside their earths, to Richmond Park with its two herds of deer, cultivated and culled to meet the

Royal Deer warrant and then on to Wimbledon Common, a handful of miles from the palace of Westminster itself.

Then there is the night's silvery lure of the Thames itself, which attracts vast populations of migrating European and Scandinavian duck onto the water and mud at Dagenham — surely one of the most unlovely waterfronts in Europe — and off the refuse heaps at Rainham Marshes where I once saw a rat so large I first thought it might have been a domestic cat. Even the sheep here turn dark-coated with the fall-out from the chimneys of the neighbouring factories. Somewhere, deep down in that reclaimed land must lie simple treasures of everyday life as these marshes were first used as refuse dumps by the Tudors.

But on the river, especially when the weather is bitter in northern Europe, are a myriad of scaup, teal, widgeon, tufted, pintail and even golden-eye ducks and a legion of mallard.

To the north there is the magnet of the river Lea with its complex of streams and lakes and the great reservoir at Walthamstow which houses one of the largest heronries in Britain. I have even charted herons flying, sometimes as high as an estimated 400 feet, from Walthamstow to the Eyots of the Thames above Richmond where I once counted forty-eight hunch-backed grey gentlemen, like a collection of gloomy lawyers, huddled on the surrounds of one Eyot alone.

The Lea glitters like a silver trail in the moonlight on cold, clear nights and entices arctic birds into London. To the west a host of small rivers and canals tempts birds down to that vast complex of reservoirs around Staines. You do not have to go up country to see crested grebes and mergansers, and this part of Middlesex now boasts the largest winter colonies of smew, the smallest and probably the most beautiful of the mergansers, in Europe, plus colonies of wintering tufted duck and pochard running into tens of thousands.

Lying in the frosted grass of a crystal dawn at Queen Mary reservoir you might easily imagine you are on the lakes of Iceland ... except that every other minute a jumbo jet rumbles out of nearby Heathrow Airport ... those waterfowl certainly have noisy neighbours and the mass of technicolor canvas of the hearty dingy sailors and sailboard experts leaping from wave-top to wave-top is regarded with evasive gloom.

Wherever I go in London, frankly an experience I now try to avoid as I hate the smell of vehicle fumes, I find things of great beauty: peering over the bridge at Kingston upon Thames as the traffic thundered mindlessly by, I watched some twenty goosanders, Europe's largest duck, almost thirty inches in height, barging through the water like a fleet of half-submerged submarines and wondered if I was the only person in the world watching them? I wasn't. Bird watchers are solitary but rarely alone.

Goosanders hunt like a wolf pack, all submerging at once and driving fish into shoal and then into shallow water where they are easier to catch and eat.

One night in summer I was walking the old dog round a well-treed square in Kensington where I was followed by an inquisitive tawny owl. He flew silently from tree to tree, sometimes behind us, sometimes overtaking us in his enthusiasm, often hardly at arm's length above my head, keeping his wide and blinking eyes on my Basset hound.

Two girls in evening dress, seeing a man loitering in the dark, the lamps were shaded by the great plane trees which edged the railed private garden, wisely crossed the road. At that moment the tawny let out its characteristic wobbly whoopee. The girls hitched up their skirts and cantered round the square towards the bright lights and safety of Knightsbridge, and I hurried away before the police arrived. They are not a very imaginative lot and I doubt very much whether they would have believed my tale of a nocturnal companion with wide brown eyes.

I later read that the tawnies, being at the head of the food chain, were found to be dying in the gardens of Kensington and examination of their corpses showed that they were killed by accumulations of insecticides. That is no way to treat an urban owl, and is no way to treat an urban garden, either. It has that distant ring of idiot logic in a scientific survey of the three main species of mice which live on the verges and central reservations of motorways. There was no evidence, the survey said, that mice died of lead poisoning even though the lead content in their vital organs was abnormally high and lead accumulations on their pelage through creeping through contaminated verge grass was also very high. Mice simply die of old age before the lead kills them. But nobody looked at the kestrels which prey on the verge mice . . .

You will not find an insecticide or a spray in my garden shed. I sit here mesmerised by my gardeners, a pink miasma of long-tailed tits working my rose bushes. They come up to the window as I write, less than two feet from my face, and gaze at me with the astonishment the Lilliputians must have expressed at Gulliver. I have also noticed the increasing number of gold-crested wrens which over-summer south of the Thames. They flit about in the bay hedge, so small that you think you are seeing things, hallucinating like the classic alcoholic who sees imaginary spiders running up the walls. But no, you are not deluded; there they are in suburban London, chattering amongst themselves as if they are the most important birds in the world . . . and they are, if you love beauty for its own sake.

Another good reason for not poisoning city gardens is the huge number of hedgehogs fussing down the pavements of night-time London, rustling the leaves in front gardens. I freely admit that the spaniel and I are hedgehog poachers. He picks them up in his mouth as a cat carries kittens and I am hardly surprised at that because he retrieves eggs laid in the grass — secreted for brooding over is probably a better description — by our runabout hens. His for certain is a tender mouth.

I simply roll the hedgies into a ball and carry them home and put them in the back garden which always needs someone, or something, to keep the pests in hand.

But here is a gentle trick you can play on city birds. Move your cage of nuts a foot or so towards your windows every other day, then into the window, or, better still patio doors, and then, if you can stand the cold, into the room. The woodpecker in his red and black lord mayor's uniform thrashes into my sitting room with the brief dazzle of a meteor burning itself out on the edges of the night sky. He steals a nut, and whooshes out again to lodge it in the crevasses in the bark of the pear tree where he hammers at it like a road mender with a pneumatic drill. The nuthatch dithers nervously, upside down, the blue tits flutter about like dandelion seed on the breeze or try to attack their own images reflected in the wall of glass.

The greatest triumph of temptation was to lay a line of bird seed and crushed dog biscuit so that a jay, to my mind the British parrot for his raucous colours, came jumping into my kitchen. Now this most cautious and careful of birds waits for the basset to finish his breakfast so that he can "clean the plate". Jays, jackdaws and magpies . . . opportunists to a fault.

There is another paradox about London which intrigues me.

I am one of those people who enjoy the social anachronism of belonging to what is popularly known as a "gentleman's club" in St James's Street. I am a country member. Amongst the dark city suits, I, in my tweeds and (usually muddy) field shoes am my own anachronism.

"You look as if you have just come up from the country," they say. Once I tried to explain why I was dressed as I was, but I soon stopped . . . an agricultural fair is as alien to them as insurance broking is to me.

But there is a warm sensation in entering the club. It has that warm country house smell; it is just sufficiently scruffy to feel lived in; it is to me, home from home. Once you close that door you shut out the real world. For some it is a refuge from nagging wives, demanding girlfriends and the wretched world of urban violence. And all the clubs are different. I know this because friends take me to other clubs occasionally: the Cavalry and Guards is spotlessly clean, as polished as a Grenadier's boots, the equestrian statuary both masterpieces of art and memories of the horrors of war. The members' dining room is noisy, as noisy as the officers' mess and sometimes as rowdy. Buck's is like a small country house with chintzy armchairs, and I expect the doors to burst open and a host of squealing children and spaniels to come tumbling in. The "In and Out" frightens me; the rooms are so vast that I feel I am living in Blenheim Palace. My own home is rather more modest than that.

There are moments of high comedy: I took a master craftsman, a cabinet maker and restorer of some renown in the county to my club. Entering the club he suddenly shouted, "Good heavens, just look at that beautiful piece of William and Mary . . ." In a trice it was upside down and he was examining it minutely. Then he had the drawers out, then he licked his fingers and rubbed the surface. "Wonderful walnut veneer," he said.

William and Mary? I think, for all the members knew, it could have been Stanley and Jennifer.

But the real prize of this club is that we have a long cad's table, a cad being a member who calls at the club to seek the company and conversation of other unattached members. The rule at the table is that you sit within talking distance of other members already seated, or they join you if you are alone. (For the misanthropic there is a line of tables where, seated with your back to the wall — it is called "The Brook" but no-one remembers why — you may scowl at those who waste their time in idle chatter.) Or you may read a book or newspaper without fear of interruption.

Seated at cad's table at any time may be peers of the realm, members of the Commons, military men, giants of industry and a good cross section of modestly successfully men on wholly egalitarian terms with each other. Conversation covers all the topics of the day; politics and finance, racing and hunting, international relations and, inevitably, gardening. We are a nation of gardeners.

Sometimes a subject, usually political, engulfs the table in furious arguments, but there is nothing which seems to inflame the passions of men at that table so much as ... the making of garden compost. It is a subject on which we are all, in our own eyes at least, the world's leading expert and everyone else's system is impossibly wrong, unworkable, detrimental to good gardening and so undesirable as to be beneath consideration.

How do you make compost break down? Well, they say, you add this or you add that. But we, the real compost makers, know what makes vegetable matter break down. When no-one is about we pee on the compost heap; it is universally acknowledged in the country that this is the correct way to start the break-down. In Victorian England gardeners collected the chamber pots from the maids in the grand houses for this purpose and when the compost was well rotted down they planted their marrows into the compost heap, and fine marrows they must have been.

So, if you multiply the number of self-appointed experts around that table to the ultimate point there must be about ten million compost experts in Britain, with his own unfailing method, stoutly defended and held with unguarded contempt for everyone else's compost. There is even one man who made compost for his window boxes at his Chelsea flat. Not only are we a nation of gardeners, we are a nation of dedicated gardeners.

The recollection of these animated conversations came to mind when we were making bread at home. Provided with exactly the same ingredients; strong flour, milk, yeast, water, salt and taking the same time to knead, raise and bake the bread, my wife's bread floated into frothy loaves which would have kept a ploughman going all day. Mine were so hard or strodgy they would have sunk an aircraft carrier. You eat my bread at risk of being awake all night with indigestion. My wife said that bread making is in the hands, and if you have not got the hands you cannot be taught.

Bread-making and brewing, as my expert neighbour had proved in companionship with his brewster wife — brewing in the country house was traditionally women's work — is not an art, nor is it a science. It is what in previous centuries was known as "a mystery".

This is the mystery we are all in danger of forgetting as we sit around Cad's or any other table: we are all most certainly born equal and we are equally born different. You may teach mathematics to a receptive mind, but not to me; you may teach ballet to an athletic body, but not to me. My mysteries are, in the best sense of the word, peculiar and individual to me. As yours are to you.

The ratchet of the egalitarian society clicks ever forward, usually not by demand of the majority but by imposition of the minority, in trying to eliminate these differences. Two steps forward before the freedom fighters of the mind can grasp one peg back against the forces of grey conformity which are fortified by an omnipresent State of immense power, and which rarely admits it can do any wrong. It has wealth — yours to use against you, remember governments do not have any money of their own — and weapons such as the Equal Opportunities Commission and the Commission for Racial Equality to ensure that equality is imposed by statute.

Down here anyone who makes a well-cut ditch, layers a hawthorn or elm-runner hedge or lays a perfect and ornamental thatch is the source of admiration and praise. How can I possibly be equal to them?

That is why, in the country, anyone who advocates a political system based on equality is seen to be probably not a liar or a fool but a clever person with ambitions towards totalitarianism. In fact, those states which claim social equality — the elimination of differences between individuals — usually have social barriers so harsh they would not be tolerated in the British countryside, as witness the ownership of Rolls Royces and the creation of a public school based overtly on Eton, in the USSR.

We should be exploiting, and I mean that word in its original sense, the essential differences between people for their personal benefit and in the national interest.

What opened my eyes to this idea was when a government agency, one of the few which had anything approaching creative ideas, showed a flash of genius in trying to exploit the inherent talents — and I mean the fundamental differences between some young people and others — in the unlikely area of them bringing severely handicapped children into contact with horses as a therapy.

These young people, at Great Barr, Birmingham, and mainly brought in from the Walsall area, still the country's centre for making metal work for the equestrian world, never for a moment dreamed of working with horses and even less of working with mentally handicapped children. Most of them admitted that they did not recognise a horse from a number "36" bus and when I asked one girl, on a cheerless morning in a muddy field, what she would be doing if she were not out here in the rain, she said: "Standing at the back door of the supermarket waiting for the next stacker's job to come up."

But this experience unlocked the mystery of their talent and we ended up with girls experienced in horse management, a couple went into nursing these unfortunate children and some went home vowing never to look at a horse or a handicapped child ever again. It was the accidental incident of unemployment which provided the opportunity. In times of full employment they might all have been competing for shop girls' jobs.

So, back to the compost and the bread-making and brewing, remembering that other's methods are not necessarily better than your own. They are simply different and it is our ability, or lack of it, to identify these mysteries which allows us to see what makes each individual so unique.

CHAPTER
FIVE

A Life of Quiet, Enchanted and Uneventful Bliss

You think we live a life of quiet, enchanted and uneventful bliss down here in the country, don't you? Well, let me put you right.

For sixty and then some years the family owned a series of fields which sloped gently upwards towards the distant downs in the west. On the side bordering the sea were cliffs, never higher than thirty feet falling away into a undercliff thick with pruned stumps of willows cut as withies for the making of lobster and prawn pots. Amongst these withies are thick black swamps and an ever increasing and inpenetrable jungle of briars. And you could bet your best black hat that at least once a year a dreamy steer, browsing along the cliff edge, would topple over. Down he would go, seven hundredweight of rump steak and brisket, crashing through the briars, into the stinking swamp, knocking down the withies to emerge shaking his head, dazed and bewildered on the beach.

Small boys would come running to tell us about this excitement, which did not rate in their anthologies quite as high as a stable fire, but much higher than a coaster aground on Bembridge ledge. We had a special lasso for these emergencies. You simply dropped it over the steer's head, it had been polled as a calf, and then it was led, docilely along the beach and back into the field.

Miraculously, over all those years, no bullock was ever injured. But not this friesian; he took to the water and stood there up to his shoulders in the sea puffing like an engine in steam. My brother, well up to his chest in water, was gently trying to drop the lasso over the steer's head without setting him off on a marathon swim in the general direction of the Nab Tower.

At that moment a small and innocent nephew came striding along the beach with all the self importance small boys can muster. "Hullo, Uncle George," he piped in his reedy voice. "Are you teaching that bullock to swim?" And you think we live a life of quiet, enchanted and uneventful bliss down here, do you?

The east end of the orchard, not even large enough to aggrandise itself as a paddock, was a jungle of neglect. While we picked the ever diminishing number of apples, the grass and wild flowers grew. Even the goat could not cope with the proliferation of rough grass, although her appetite for brambles was endless and it sent shivers down my spine to watch her eating the brambles, thorns and all.

A four-wheeled rotary mower was borrowed and I soon discovered that you needed the strength of a team of horses to handle it. But the mower battered down the grass under which lived an over-populated city of field mice, some voles and the occasional shrew. Complicated runs, the motorways of the mouse world, inter-connected this quarter acre and I sat in the chewed up grass looking at what might be, for the animal kingdom, their own motorways, crossroads and even Spaghetti Junction.

Then there were the little balls, almost architectural in their symmetry, which were the town and country houses of the mice . . . in fact, the nests in which the blind, pink young, no bigger than your thumb nail, were born and remained until their blind eyes could see the light, and the dangers, of the world. I opened up several of these perfections to make sure there were no "babes in arms" in them.

The dog Rex, a Welsh Springer spaniel, and in my opinion the only dog in the world to have an IQ of minus ten, killed the mice by the hundred. You could see the glee on his face. Animal death to animal death to my mind is acceptable, that is the way the natural world made itself and, despite the harsh and thoughtless hand of man, continues to survive.

The kestrel, usually "At home" on the tip of a telegraph pole, will surely not starve. There must be a million mice in the next few acres and on the cliff edges. And even though the life-span of a field mouse is only about three months in the wild, the million that die today will be replaced by another million tomorrow.

I sat in the grass pondering these things and came to the conclusion that it would pay me to employ a gardener because it takes me a day to do what he could achieve in an hour and at a quarter of the cost.

Sitting there, I started looking at the grass itself. Here was another prolific colonisation of great beauty which can never be seen on well barbered lawns. The expected were all present: Perennial rye-grass, Common couch, Sea couch — we are only a hundred yards from the beach — Italian rye, many barleys and cord, but there were some unexpected visitors amongst the yarrow and the American usurper, the Rose-bay willow herb. I am sure that some of these flowers were escapees from private gardens: a dazzling red figwort and a flower I know only under the name of Solomon's seal. But when I discovered clumps of sea thrift I decided it was high time to get back to work and really earn my mid-day thirst.

I took the riphook to the hedge. On the second slash the air was inflamed with the noise of a racing car revving on the starting grid, and the wild bees thundered out of their suspended nest, which hung like a vast brown pear, to investigate this murderous intruder . . . except that he was not there. He had already set off at undignified speed out of the orchard.

During the afternoon while I was mashing another area of grass to pulp — the orchard was, in fact, reverting back to scrub and eventually, if time had allowed, into woodland — the mower disturbed a subterranean nest of "Humble bees" which erupted from the ground like a continuous launching pad of humming space-probes. I know they are not dangerous as I often handle them in the same way that I put cold bumble

70

bees, whose sting can be very painful, into my hands to warm them up after a cold or wet night. But I made off again, this time out of courtesy.

My peace, reading a book about wild flowers — I think the three varieties of plantain are amongst the most beautiful of wild flowers (I do not mind if you call them weeds) and the Great plantain is the best of the lot — and also talking to the half-witted spaniel, was ruined first by the grinding of a lorry and then the sudden crashing of lime stone for walling being tipped.

Lorry drivers are an odd lot. It is their job to deliver stone. This he did. He opened the five-barred gate to the drive, reversed into it. Then he drove quickly away, his mission completed to his entire satisfaction. The stone entirely blocked the drive.

Dressed in two bandana handkerchiefs knotted at the waist I started moving the stone . . . all twelve tons of it; half a ton in the morning, half a ton each afternoon and all in fierce sunshine. It was just as well I was not planning on going anywhere in the car . . . With perspiration running off me like a cascade I felt my muscles rippling by the end of the week. Tarzan, I thought, you should see me now! I felt so fit and well, my food tasted so much better, I crept into bed and slept a dreamless sleep like a pig in clean straw. I drank up my cider, which in this vintage had been made from proper, little red bitter apples which produced pink rather than straw-coloured cider, cider rosé so to speak, and discovered a profound fact: that if you turn fat into muscle you put on weight.

With all these chores achieved by the weekend I decided to relax. I sprawled in bed reading and I heard, unmistakably, the scampering of rats up the insides of the wall and across the rafters in the roof. It is a simple fact of rural life that if you have animal food you will eventually have rats. They must be destroyed.

Other than monkeys they carry the greatest number of zoonotic diseases, diseases conveyed from animal to human, than any other British mammal. The damage they do and the spoiling of both animal and human food is horrendous. Total war must be declared. By comparison, incidentally, our good friends, the fox and the badger, carry few zoonotic diseases, but they are the last repository of something we can all do without: humans have, in the last half century, become so clean and well scrubbed that the human flea no longer can be found on humans, but foxes and badgers not only have their own fox and badger fleas but human fleas as well.

So the planned day of leisure was spent with the half-wit spaniel, who quickly proved that he had only been faking and that behind that gormless grin and a deep desire to ingratiate himself was a keen and analytical mind, equal to that of any ratting terrier. He really has got brains, it is just that he likes to coast through life without making too much of an effort.

Soon we were following the runs, the rats had actually burrowed under the foundations of the house. Then there was the baiting and the setting of traps, a visit to the village to buy some kippers as there is no rat in the world which can resist the unique smell of kippers — and then, the

72

next morning the checking of the traps at the house, in the barns and by the kennels.

It took only three days. There are no rats in the house now I can assure you, and even the spaniel has earned the smug smile he wears on his mistakenly stupid face.

And you think that we live a life of quiet, enchanted and uneventful bliss down here in the country. If I wanted that sort of life I would get a job in a bank . . . and I might even get paid for it.

Now that the chores were really over I knew I could devote a couple of days to riotous living and unconfined joy, so with Benjamin between the shafts we bowled down the lane at almost reckless pace. On forty-eight inch, sixteen-spoke wheels and rubber tyres the ralli trap has only to hit a stone the size of a hen's egg and we are like Mad Jack Mytton, the early nineteenth-century Shropshire squire — you remember him, he was the one who set fire to his nightshirt to cure the hiccups and to prove that he was not afraid of "my brother fire" — who said to his travelling companion, "Was you never upset in a gig?"

The man nervously said, "No", and Mad Jack promptly ran a wheel up the bank, capsized the cart and threw both of them heavily into the lane.

But my brother is a master of the ribbons — and shows a little more common sense in holding the headstrong Benjamin, wrongly named after the least of the tribes of Israel, to a steady trot. Come the hills and I have to climb over my seat, open the rear gate and jump out of the back to lighten the load so that the pony does not have to break pace. At the brow of the hill I clamber up the two iron steps and into my seat. Benjamin trots on . . . I gasp for breath.

A ralli is made for speed. We put the children into a governess cart, especially constructed very deep so that mummy's precious ones will not easily fall out. Their heads pop up above the boards like coconuts at a fairground and Benjamin's mother takes them down the same lane at a matronly walk.

We had the ralli, the governess cart, two tubs and a London trolley, all found forgotten and neglected in scrap and builder's yards. You can buy them new cheaper at places such as Hay on Wye and Peterborough, but we wanted the fun of rebuilding antique vehicles, as much as anything to see how they were originally put together. Knock the wheels off and under the knaves of the brass hubs they are often dated and marked with their home town. Our tubs, to our surprise, were Dublin, 1890s. However and why did they ever get to the Isle of Wight?

But we had to have new wheels made. A local carpenter steamed and formed the elm boards to rebuild three vehicles, stroked five coats of paint on each board and although he was a young man with a prodigious appetite for beer drew a perfect yellow line freehand to our regal blue traps. They were now a wonder to the eye.

But our nearest wheelwright is at Ashford, Kent; an amazing treasure house of wood and spokes, sawdust, shavings, rubber and metal tyres and tools so strange in design that you can only wonder at their purpose.

But here was the rub: we were a long way down the list and would have to wait for some weeks before our wheels could be rebuilt. Driving has become such a popular pastime, perhaps as a subconscious rebellion against the auto-age and the all-destructive motorway. But the result is that many craftsmen are overwhelmed with work.

So, down to Reading I went, where I found, in bizarre fashion at least, that the spirit of Dick Turpin lives on, but in reality to see what I might find at a spectacular sale of vehicles. "Horse drawn vehicles are the perfect example of British eccentricity on show," the auctioneer, a national authority on horse drawn vehicles and author on this delightful subject, said as the rain came bursting down the wind in wild tumults and we cradled our cups of tea to warm our hands.

And what a collection: a Kent Van, Phaetons, a Chair Back Gig, a Basket Pony Chaise actually made of woven wickerwork and of such dottiness that you wanted to laugh out loud or sneak back and take another look to make sure Queen Victoria had not climbed aboard (it sold for a fortune, of course) an American Buckboard Phaeton, a Park Drag and a huge number of vehicles so rotten and eaten away by worm and the rot of ages you were frightened to sneeze in case they fell to pieces.

But as long as you have the axles and can measure the length and height and remove the ironwork, the most vauable parts of these vehicles, your restored trap would be as good as Abraham Lincoln's "original" axe with five new handles and three new heads.

I hurried off to have a good look at "Quicksilver", possibly the most famous of all the stage coaches which blustered down the roads of Britain before the railways gradually drove them out of business. Not only did the Quicksilver live up to her name by holding the staging Blue Riband, London to Devonport in under nineteen hours (with one twenty minute stop for refreshments en route), but she was designed with a low centre of gravity, to prevent swaying, complicated springing and oiled hub boxes. The most famous coachmen of their days, held in the same awe as motor-racing drivers are today, took the ribbons with six horses up front — I can assure you that driving a four requires every moment of your concentration, plus arms of steel, so what these leviathans of the roads must have been like at speed is almost beyond imagination.

I climbed inside to see if I could discover something of that distant magic, but the first thought, one which had come to mind in other places, was that however sophisticated Quicksilver might have been, it must have been bone-achingly uncomfortable. The other thought was that people, everyone in general, must have been on average very much smaller than modern man, perhaps not in height, but certainly across the hips and shoulders.

I had this thought when looking at the tragic uniform of Nelson at Greenwich, at Wellington's uniforms and especially at the spectacular dresses of lady courtiers to the Stuarts now in the Victoria and Albert Museum. If the dresses are a reasonable guide these fashionable ladies must, by modern standards, have been midgets.

Perhaps the pendulum of growth has swung all the way back: the "Duke" of Essex, who commanded the

76

"English" forces at the famous battle of Maldon in 991 in the years of Aethelred II, was estimated to be 6ft 9in tall from the measurement of his bones when his tomb in the singing beauty of Ely Cathedral were opened in 1969.

And on the Isle of Wight, when a Druid era mass grave, possibly the site of a ritualistic slaughter, was opened, it was found that all the skeletons were of men well over six feet.

Then appeared the spectre of Master Turpin: one of the highlights of the Reading auction was a square backed gig renovated to an immaculate show finish in royal blue with red lining and black leather trim. It was knocked down for a mere £2,950 and at the end of the day its new owner came to take it home . . . only to find that it had been spirited away.

Horse drawn vehicles are a natural adjunct of country life because if you have animals you will have horse-, donkey-, Shetland-drawn carts. If you don't believe me take a trip to Chatsworth House in Derbyshire where there is a miniature vehicle so ornate, so strange that it is almost like a waking nightmare but which is a child's cart designed to be drawn . . . by a goat. Try that on our goat and see what happens to you.

But it is not always the great things in our lives, the eccentricities of donkeys, the dreams of rattling down the turnpikes, the stubborn cows that make up the dramas in our lives. Sometimes there are little things which bring smiles of sweet surrender to the wild things of this world.

I had been up in the roof where I had previously dealt with those wretched rats and I had left the roof hatch open — you could furnish another complete house with all the "handy gubbins" we have collected over the years and tucked away for another day — and I could hear a distant whispering and a strange but very small noise as if someone was dragging his finger nails over a sheet of paper. Out of bed I got, yet again, and armed with a torch, I climbed the loft ladder and slowly and cautiously poked my head into the darkness before switching on the torch. On one wall was a small grey mass, like a moving growth of fungus: bats.

As the autumn progressed — there were days of endless sunshine as the light yellowed and faded like a piece of ancient parchment, the nights grew colder; no clouds above to hold the day's heat — the body corporate of bats slowly but steadily increased.

Like almost everyone else, and this includes many country people, I knew nothing about bats. They were just pleasant little creatures which skimmed about the house and garden at twilight when the day-time skimmers, the swallows and martins, had gone to roost and the swifts were nodding off on the wing.

The bats in my roof seemed to chatter endlessly amongst themselves and wriggle about as they crowded together in hibernation, and as winter went by I would hold my hands near their bodies, like small and over-ripe grey plums, and feel them getting colder.

There were no bats in the roof of my house near London although there were plenty of accesses, entrances and exits under the eaves, and even though they populated the river where there were millions of small flying insects and where there is a huge colony in Hammersmith amongst the streets of fading houses fortunately for the bats kept in bad repair, and where they are now more than adequately protected by law.

I began to love the bats and discovered that they had perfected themselves 50 million years ago when man was hardly more than an ape. I have often wondered why we have accumulated so many prejudices about one of the largest, most beautiful and intelligent of the families of the little kingdom we disparagingly call "animal".

But now the bats have gone. And so have most of the visiting tawnies from the London garden. Went in a single night and although you could hear the trees crashing down from end to end of the parish, twenty six limes in all, plus inoffensive whitebeams and hawthorns, the significance of our loss was not immediately understood.

We think Sir Christopher Wren planted the avenue — the first line is horse chestnuts followed by four lines of limes to make what I believe is the second longest avenue in Britain. It was amazing to look into the entrails of the now stranded whales of those horse chestnuts and limes for the meagre remnants of the tawnies' homes — you could put the entire makings of their nest in one hand — before the lean woodsmen parcelled the trees into firewood.

The bats left nothing that I could find and I walked back to the house with only an armful of previously unobtainable mistletoe, some with branches thicker than your thumb and, of course, completely out of season,

Christmas having long since slipped into memory. But the policeman got off his bike and looked at me sideways. I expect there is a statute somewhere or other about taking mistletoe during its close season . . .

The bats used to come and look at us as we sat in the gathering darkness under the great Caucasian oak, which created its own premature dusk at the furthest end of the garden. An uncountable number of flying insects performed their last pavane for our silent friends to create their acrobatics over our heads.

But there was a game, now entirely lost to us. If you waved a white handkerchief above your head the bats, little chaps that you could put into the palm of your hand, came down within inches of your face to investigate.

The children shrieked — and how they enjoyed all that shrieking — and ran to sanctuary near the house or into the familiar safety of the kitchen. Soon they crept out; soon they wanted to wave or throw the handkerchief. The ladies, conditioned by generations of myths about bats flying into the hair, all utterly untrue as there is no single historic or authenticated record of this ever having happened, fled to the house where they made vows never to forgive my tricks.

In a sad way their fears have come true. I now find it difficult to find bats anywhere. They used to come out at noon in harsh sunshine in the middle of July under the darkness of a line of cupressus. Under the giant conker trees at Ham House on the edge of the Thames they were oblivious of the stench and bustle of the accumulation of polo ponies and the busy grooms in the heat of the afternoon.

Unlike urban foxes and badgers and the hordes of feral cats, the bats have not coped with our world. Some fly, some seem to flutter as delicately as moths, and we all have the most desperately wrong illusions about their spooky abilities. How fast did they fly round the ladies' heads as they zoomed out of the darkness? Try something just above ten miles an hour in level flight and that sustained for only a few seconds. Even the maximum in this country is believed to be no more than thirteen miles an hour.

In deep railway cuttings in Dorset where there are some of the last great colonies of the Horseshoe bat they are killed by express trains, like moths on the windscreen of a car; because although they can hear the train approaching they cannot estimate its speed or get out of the way in time.

But there may be a small ray of hope where the perversity of man may help our harmless friends. It has been seen that large colonies of bats roost on the supporting girders of bridges over the terrifying multi-lane highways in some of the southern states of America, particularly in California. They are safe, and unseen from above . . . and only a lunatic would stray onto those lethal highways.

We walked up our fields with that serene host of in-whelp greyhounds and there, hanging on the wire in the wind and cold drizzle, was a bat. It was so small, with a ferocious face, huge ears, its leather wings folded away with the complicated formality of an umbrella; it was an old animal and it was dying.

81

The children shrieked — shrieking does not seem to do children much harm — and the bat was borne home from the cold wintery field so that it could be cared for. At first no small eyes would look at our aged invalid. Then they came back and cautiously peered into the box, then they wanted to touch, to hold, to cradle our dying friend. His tiny and ugly face became a thing of great beauty and when he died, within the hour, the children fell unusually silent. They went into empty rooms to play on their own.

There is an answer: I have ensured that there are openings in the roof in case the bats ever come back and want to stay. So far the reward for our charity was an infestation of wasps which made a huge nest like an oriental lampshade and promptly stung everyone. They had to go.

Then there were deep deliberations about the buying or making of bat boxes where they can live and breed and where they can hibernate; sizes and temperatures were regarded as critical as was height and the direction in which the boxes faced. Heads were stuck in books, learned journals were consulted, wise men talked to.

It must be true that you cannot feel a loss for something you have never experienced. But those children who shrieked and ran off to hide from the bats will soon have children of their own, and I would hate it if they came into a world in which innocent games cannot be played with fierce-faced, flying friends in the garden.

And you think we live a life of quiet, enchanted and uneventful bliss down here in the country. Let me put you right.

CHAPTER
SIX

Eating Out

The gardener had peeled an onion about half the size of a football and he was eating it like an apple. If you had struck a match I am sure his breath would have caught fire except that I could hardly see to strike anything as the onion tears ran down my cheeks.

"Whatever are you doing?" I pleaded.

"Beginning to get a cold," he said. "This'll keep it off. Then tonight I rubs my chest with garlic and covers it with felt and in the morning I 'as a spoon of honey and I'm right as rain. 'Aven't 'ad a proper cold in twenty years," he added proudly . . . and very few friends, I thought, if you smell like that. Thank goodness he works out of doors, alone, year round, round year.

His chat set me thinking about a remark made by a home brewer, one of those men with a face with as many lines and more colours than the little map of the London Underground you find at the back of every diary. He said that with dextroses, lactoses, riboflavin, and a host of other vitamins and insoluble enzymes beer drinkers rarely got colds or influenza. He should know, he is living proof of his own theory; he tucks away at least eight pints a day, and the only time he has been ill in the last twenty-five years was from an ailment more common in horses than men.

Certainly over the years there has been a gradual rediscovery not only of herbalism in both medicine — you have already guessed that I am interested in this mystery — and cosmetics but also in homeopathic medicine, generally understood as the use of natural poisons to battle against bodily poisons.

All in fact that we are doing is going through the continuous process of rediscovering the mysteries of plants which have been used since ancient times but which were washed away with the drift to the cities, the revolution of the "ordered garden" and the monopoly of medicine in the hands of the educated few. But go back to the old cottage garden — if you can still find one — and you will quickly discover that country people live on the borderline between the cultivation of proprietary garden plants and "weeds". Weeds are often quite rightly quoted as "flowers in the wrong place" and most of us try not to distinguish between the two.

A piece of sour ground, especially if it is well fertilised with a high nitrogen manure such as a disused chicken-run, throws up a thick crop of nettles, but who makes nettle soup today (or better still nettle and lime leaf soup), now cuts young nettles as spinach, reaps it for digging into light land as you would dig in comfrey or sunflower stems. At one time nettles were part rotted to make a short-staple flax.

Half the problem of convincing people that wild foods are edible is to overcome some of history's cock-eyed ideas: that a poppy head on a human head is a curative because they are the same shape. It works best on the human head when it is the opium poppy, but I do not recommend that you play about with it. Or there was the idea that a flower with an "eye" like my Black-eyed Susans, were curative for human eyes.

There is no doubt that some flowers, weeds if you insist, are useful in flower (wine), fruit, stem and root and leaves; how could we have given up the blanching of dandelions with silver sand or collecting the young green leaves and mixing them with fried bacon and bacon fat to make the classic dish, *Pis en lit*, which is eaten by my town friends like greedy piglets at the milk-bar. And then to have replaced it by milk-sop lettuce . . .

But where do we start? First of all put out of mind, for the time being at least, Chinese potions which need dragon's bones and bear's bile. These appear to be in short supply round here at present. Think that there are something like 2,250,000 known plants in the world. (It is easily possible to understand, incidentally, that some plants will be created, develop and slip into oblivion without human eyes ever lighting on them.)

Before going any further I must underline that the unlearned or misused application of plants in medicine is hideously dangerous and any ideas and suggestions put forward here should be used only by skilled, experienced or qualified hands.

The contradiction is that many common, poisonous plants also have strong medicinal properties. I have always written and said, especially to the children when they were young, that yew berries are wholly poisonous.

Not true. But it was a lie worth telling if it prevented someone from becoming both very ill and painfully ill or even die. In truth, the flesh of ripe yews is very tasty; the seeds are fatal and who can trust small children not to accidentally swallow them?

Some plants achieve the right result for the wrong reasons: False hellebore, an acrid and corrosive plant, has historically been used in abortions not because it creates abortions but because it has irritant and toxic effects; and Fool's parsley has never lived up to its name for it has been used for 1,000 recorded years for a multitude of ailments; and the minute Scarlet pimpernel which proliferates and has always filled my eyes with pleasure ... to the point where I found, only recently, that the name (*Anagallis arvensis*) came from the idea that the flowers create merriment and laughter. All I can say is that it works with me.

Throughout their lives I taught the children that the Deadly nightshade (*Atropa belladonna*) is the bringer of everlasting night to humans, while my herbals describe it as one of the most important of natural drugs. But it is a narcotic poison which creates hallucinations and death, dilating the pupils, causing high flushing — a burning sensation — in the face and a fiery dry throat. Incidentally, *Belladonna mutuallis* cancels out the toxic and hallucinatory effects of the opium Poppy. But please do not try the one to test the other.

White bryony causes death by asphyxia; but you can use the milky juice to remove warts and should the occasion arise, according to Linné (*Linnaeus*), six fruits of Spurge olive, an attractive four-petalled pink flower, will kill a wolf. Unfortunately he forgot to tell us how to persuade the wolf to eat them.

But why am I so attracted to poisonous plants when I cannot even bring myself to read reports of murder and violence in the newspapers and abhor war books? Why do I love our native Foxglove, still widely used in modern medicine, when descriptions of the way it causes death make my skin creep. Incidentally, I believe it is just historically possible that unscrupulous herbalists used spurge juice, rubbed on the skin to cause sores, to prove that by touching the hem of a royal garment, as in the cure for "King's Evil" — *Scrofula* — that the monarch had magical curative powers because the sores quickly disappear without further dousings with spurge.

Other plants which combine both beauty and danger, like particularly alluring sirens tempting us to destruction, are the hellebores — the Christmas rose — the plumbagos and the common Buttercup as merely one representative of the huge ranunculus family but which is a sure-fire poison. The delightful Squill, probably the best natural diuretic known to man, is also nasty tasting and a narcotic poison.

One herbal, which must have been written tongue-in-cheek, says of hemp (*Cannabis*), which is used medicinally with tobacco to cure asthma: "When crossing hemp fields in summer at the height of the day it generally produces an intense, dizziness, giddiness and a special psychic state . . ."

I do not recommend that you grow it, even for your pet budgie, as it also produces the village constable on his bike and a magical mystery ride to the police station . . .

I was reminded of all this lore when, with a town-based friend, we were skirting a copse in the company of a motley of two Basset hounds, a Welsh springer, a Field spaniel, dogs of uncertain parentage, some of which I am sure were not ours but had invited themselves along for a stroll, when my friend said: "When I am with you in the country you are always eating."

My answer was quite simply that the food is always there. His worry was the natural one of the town dweller that he did not know which fruits, flowers, mushrooms and green plants were safe.

My mind went back to those days when I was educating the children about the many poisonous plants which lived in the orchard which had been allowed to become a wilderness. This is where the Deadly nightshade and the beautiful Black nightshade (*Solanum nigrum*), grow. I squashed their fragrant berries in my fingers, telling the smallest child, then only a tot, that five — I allowed myself to exaggerate — would kill her. "But the blackbird over there had already eaten a hundred", — she, too, is allowed to exaggerate — and he hasn't died. And if pheasants eat them, why haven't you died because you eat pheasants?' This is the irrefutable logic of childhood.

The orchard provides some other surprises. Fungi seem to appear overnight and at the most odd times of the year. Field mushrooms from the paddocks seem to behave themselves and appear at the times the textbooks say they should, although a muggy September and old pastures used by horses improves the chances of a good natural crop. These field mushrooms are brought home in my cap and are carefully examined to make sure an odd Death cap has not crept in even though we know the chances are slim. Death caps live up to their names, rarely a year goes by that someone does not die from eating this imposter which is not easy even for the experienced to distinguish from the real thing.

Then, uninvited, Parasol mushrooms appeared through the leaves under the Coxs and Blenheims. At first they were pointed charactures of themselves in their paintings in coy fairy stories, but they quickly opened up as large as soup plates. One mushroom alone filled the frying pan — they are always best cooked in bacon fat — and provided such a substantial meal I worked on the stone wall without a break until noon when cider called.

There are at least thirty species of fungi, many of which do not have common names, which may kill if eaten in sufficient quantities. Fortunately most have the courtesy of being ugly, contorted, smelly or so brightly coloured as to put temptation behind you. Quite a number, particularly the so-called dung-mushroom, are hallucinatory.

There are many common field plants and not a few which live in town gardens which one instinctively knows are wholly poisonous. For instance the garden laburnum is poisonous in every part of the plant; ivy and the yew which does not kill birds because it passes so quickly through their bodies; and those two beautiful and sought after flowers, the Fritillaries and the Lily of the valley.

But it would be a shame to miss out on those which are perfectly safe. When the children were tots, I taught them to like lime leaves for their sugary secretion. We still make lime leaf and dandelion salads — it was the Elizabethans who invented the phrase "cut 'n' come again" with their cultivation of dandelions as a vegetable.

As a result of all this plenty around me I began to wonder at the herb garden — we have sixteen species growing, all the usual ones, Rosemary, Sage, Woodland thyme, Rue, Whorehound, Lemon balm, Lavender (used for chewing to cleanse the breath). And have you filled small jars with your herbs — Rosemary is the best and most useful — and filled them with real olive oil and then painted the mature mixure, three weeks is usually long enough, on the Sunday roast lamb.

There is hardly a herb used in the preparation of meat dishes which cannot be used in this way, and Rue and Whorehound and all the other "bitters" are best used in mixed drinks if you still bother to mix cocktails, and Comfrey has limited uses in the kitchen as it has such a high alkeline content, possibly the highest amongst all readily available plants. But the herbals devote pages to its almost magical powers. (When I first grew Comfrey I thought I had mistakenly grown Indian hemp, then I thought it might be a *Nicotiana* as the first flowers are not dissimilar to tobacco, and I was relieved to find, when the leaves had matured, that I had grown the right seeds).

On the other and edible hand, there are wild cherries in the chine, but you have to be about early to get those before the blackbirds gorge themselves. They are so tart they make your tongue leap out of your head without drying your mouth like sloes. There are also wild crab apples which are too small to be of much culinary use and as sour as a nagging wife's smile. Sometimes we make a sort of jam from them, with Rowans and Whitebeam berries — it needs the apples and their pectin to make the jam set.

Always on the lookout for the unusual, I found that a friend who lives in a tudor house has a mulberry, he believes it was planted with the house and from its obvious great age and the fact that the trunk has almost faded away and is propped up with poles I am disinclined to argue with him. Mulberry jam, made when the berries are almost black, is one of life's rare delights as is quince marmalade, made from those great, eversolidly hard fruits which look like green or yellow hairy pears. They are not to be confused with juniper "quinces" which are grown ornamentally in gardens and make a jam which when made by me looks like and tastes of brown paint.

The question eventually arises as to how all these poisonous plants get into the garden and orchards. I go around removing the dangerous ones, leaving just a few as precautionary examples for my own family and neighbours who are as beset with children as we are with mice.

Then I look at the pleached hedge, which is coming along very nicely thank you, and recall immediately that it reflects very little credit on me. I am very much a second class citizen when it comes to pleached hedges, I simply do the navvying, all the hard work is done by my assistant gardeners. I topped the trees when they had grown to the correct height and I carefully remove the front and rear pointing branches, take out the alternate side branches so that the trees link arms and provide a natural fence cum hedge like an interlocked ladder. Most of the pleached hedges I have seen are of lime, largely because they are easy to work. But the under-gardeners inspired me to be different and my hedge was constructed, that is the only word, from Yew and Holly. In truth the choice of trees was made by birds, not me. I encourage birds into the garden. In one autumn week there were twenty-seven different species of them including three of my favourites: Stonechats, Bramblings and a bird no illustrated book ever portrays in its true explosion of colour, the redstart.

But my assistant gardeners are the commonplaces of country gardens, the Thrushes, Blackbirds and especially the greedy Woodpigeons. We have some eighty feet of bay hedge, all grown from seed and by that rare accident the one at the furthest end is female and was allowed to grow to its full height. The woodies settle in the bay and guzzle its black berries as if fearing there will be famine tomorrow.

The success of the birds' work is that these fruits and berries pass through them and are dropped at random around the garden from where the birds perch. The nearest fruiting yew is several hundred yards from the house, but every year a profusion of yews appear, invited or not, in every part of the garden. The hollies are even further away, but it is a constant battle taming the potential forest of hollies bird-seeded in the garden. But in the coldest part of winter it was a remarkable sight to see the holly branches bowed down with over two hundred redwings feasting and screeching like a medieval banquet.

The attraction of my garden in particular is that I have one of the tallest trees in the neighbourhood, a Caucasian oak, (*Quercus macracanthera*), which, although only planted in 1888 is now seventy feet tall with a vast canopy. And even that canopy has spread ten feet in the last fifteen years so I wonder quite where it will be when it reaches maturity at 150 to 180 years of age.

The assistant gardeners sit in this great tree while food passes through their abrasive crops, which reduces the thickness of the shells. Then there is the corrosive effect of stomach acids and the high moist temperatures which all increase the chances of germination.

But the finds are not all mundane and poisonous trees and shrubs; mahonias spring up like weeds and trip me back into childhood when we squashed the purple berries and smeared them over our naked bodies claiming we were ancient Britons daubed with woad. The only ancient thing we gained was an old fashioned smacked bottom and a visit to the vast, old fashioned cast-iron bath.

Other finds in the garden have brought lasting pleasure: a dashing *Cotoneaster frigidus* which bears fruit as big and bright as a Whitebeam's in winter while paradoxically the Whitebeam itself, the first of the fruiting trees to be ravaged, this year by flocks of starlings which are too timid to come to the pyracanthus growing against the walls of the house, shows no signs of being propagated by birds in my garden while all my friends would swear Biblical oaths that they cannot cope with bird-seeded Whitebeams. The mysterious arrival of this cotoneaster is that I, and all my neighbours, do not know of another specimen in the parish. Wherever, therefore, did it come from?

Even better was the discovery of a *Rosa rubrifolia*, which, like a coy girl, sets out in dowdy clothing — dull brown hips — and then matures into startling crimson hips, bright as redstarts, which stay on the shrub for weeks.

I grew the firethorn especially to attract the Blackbirds ... and give the seedlings away to grateful friends. And add to this profusion the wind-blown Buddleias — I have never had any success with the crimson or white varieties — and a Comfrey which appeared with immaculate precision in the only gap to be found at the back of the herb garden and you can turn the eternal mysteries of nature with a gentle hand to your own advantage.

The assistant gardeners are certainly worthy of their praise and the cost of their hire is minimal. I divide my world into those worthies who are addicted, indeed, covet crab apple jelly especially at breakfast and those Philistines who will not touch it. To indulge my one confectionary aberration a heavy fruiting John Downey variety was planted, and each year

The ouzel cock, so black of hue
with orange tawny bill . . .

as the enchanted Bottom sang in Shakespeare's ". . . Dream", arrives in his sombre aldermanic robes and feasts so enthusiastically and energetically that I wonder if the fallen apples have fermented and the Blackbirds are drunk. Is it possible to see joy on the face of a bird? I am beginning to think so.

As I walk up the narrow and steep sided valley between East and West woods with the usual motley of dogs and children, I see the game keeper creeping about along the hedge on his hands and knees. He has a beard like Moses, a nose the colour of a bird cherry — and you should see the Blackbirds eat those minute fruits so that in one year I counted three hundred seedlings under one tree alone — and his lined face is incongruously surmounted by national health specs, and a bald head the colour of a burnished mahogany piano lid. But what is he doing?

Gardening, of course. Setting out some culinary delights.

He is planting *Cotoneaster horizontalis* and what he calls "Oregon grapes", our old friend the mahonia. The tempting red and purple berries growing on the edges of his coverts ensure that his precious and very expensive reared pheasants do not stray off to other estates in the autumn for food . . . and I can easily understand his way of thinking about eating out.

All that is the practical, almost pragmatic interpretation of wild and garden plants and flowers. I am wary of any romantic view of flowers and I have the deepest of suspicions about the language of flowers. I am beginning to think that the whole vocabulary is a concoction possibly created, and certainly honed, by love-lorn Victorian lasses in their boredom.

You also have to be careful not to confuse spurious human characteristics — anthropomorphism is the worse fault in naturalists — and emotions attributed to flowers with the material properties that plants and flowers may have in the hands of skilled herbalists.

I refuse to believe that the gift of Wild tansy is a "declaration of war" as folklore would have it; a handful of dandelions "rustic oracle"; or a ragwort complete with cinnabar caterpillars would be much more insulting. And why should Rusticia be an expression that your lady friend is the perfection of female loveliness, or wolfsbane mean "misanthrophy"? Can the African marigold really mean "a vulgar mind"? I take exception to this — my garden is full of them.

All this came back to me in those ancient woods near Ockley, where Surrey and Sussex roll gently into love with each other. (While I was looking at the trees my lady was looking, surreptitiously, at farms).

So we sat in silence, watching the smoke-haze on the quiet hills. Suddenly the sun broke through and some of the trees were dipped in golden light while others stood in deep gloom.

All the primitive fears came rushing back: we were not watching the trees — the trees were watching us. The language of flowers may well be bogus, enhanced by Georgian and Victorian dreamers; but the language of trees, now long since unspoken south of the border unless there is an embodiment of it in Welsh, is historically real and in practical use today. In every country in western Europe from Iceland, through Scandinavia to the Greek islands and for all I know in Africa and Asia where I have not travelled, trees are a fundamental ingredient of pagan religion and folklore and have been bowdlerised into the modern fairy stories of Hans Andersen and the Grimm brothers.

John Evelyn, the quaint and quacky seventeenth-century antiquarian and diarist, put his finger on the truth when he was lamenting that he had outlived his age: the rationality imposed on the nation by Cromwell's Commonwealth drove witchcraft and lore out of the countryside, largely by the worst of all means, the impostion of fear even in the practice of benign witchcraft, which far outweighed the malign, so that much of the rich heritage of country tales and the words and phrases by which they were expressed were lost. Now, to find the sources of our most ancient written language we have to go back to Roman and Romano-British works.

The language was lost, lost forever. But long "Before the Roman came to Rye or out to Severn strode . . ." the Druids were devising not only a language based on their worship of trees, but an alphabet which has seeped into the English language. (I doubt if the Druids would have been happy with the Victorian definition of mistletoe, "I surmount difficulties".)

It is an alphabet of great beauty and consists of the usual five vowels but only thirteen consonants. But what is cunning about the tree alphabet is that it corresponds with the leafing or flowering of each tree as the months of the year pass ... there are thirteen months in the lunar year.

It starts with the earliest leafing tree, the Birch (Beth — letter B), through the Rowan, the Tree of Life, still known as "The Witch" in some parts — and reputedly used by the Druids to compel demons to answer the most difficult questions or suffer exquisite tortures, then the Ivy, Dwarf elder and Elder which holds its fruit into what we know as December.

What is striking are the easy similarities between the southern Druidic language and both the ancient and modern Gaelic alphabet of Beth — Luis — Nain and its equals throughout Europe.

It is true to say that the letters of the modern Irish alphabet are entirely based on the Druids' reverence for trees except that in pronunciation the letter A has become the Elm, as in the Gaelic, O the broom and T the gorse.

The new Gaelic alphabet consists of eighteen letters, all represented by a tree, and which possibly explains why the English find the language so difficult to learn.

But can we take it further? Can we believe the myths of trees are still with us? Can bewitched horses — and there are plenty of them about — only be controlled with a whip made of Rowan? I can easily believe that the letter H, pronounced "scathe" as in "scatheless" and representing the month of May, also represented a time when people were admonished to go about in their oldest clothes.

"Ne'er cast a clout till May be out ..."

Those Druids knew a thing or two, but we seem to have inherited only the catchphrases, not the reasoning. The reasoning is simple, although it may have become distorted through the oral tradition down the ages and misty centuries — you cannot even be sure that the original Latin transcriptions are accurate.

Each tree had a magic power or was used for divination or was directly associated with the god who lived inside the tree or perhaps, like the great god Thor himself, took refuge in its branches. Even Christian saints such as Wilfred or Boniface achieved fame or martyrdom through their contact with tree worshippers.

The creepiest story in the Druid calendar is naturally reserved for the thirteenth month, R (Ruis for Elder). There is reputed to be a legend told until recently in Britain that a babe put into an elder-wood cradle might easily pine away to nothing or be mercilessly pinched by fairies. The traditional wood for cradles is birch, which signifies the birth of the new year. (Please never forget that Christmas was, for centuries, celebrated in March as a Festival of Light as the days grew longer and the infant Christ represented the hopes of new growth and plenty.)

That is the language of the trees. There is nothing accidental about it.

I turned and looked back into the darkening wood. Occasionally a woodmouse rattled the dry, dry leaves in search of beech mast. But for the rest, silence. Complete silence which hung in the stillness of the autumn evening. Silence is my friend. But did I, for just one fleeting moment feel real terror amongst the trees? Was I, for that moment, at one with my Druid ancestors?

After all, John the Baptist adopted the pre-Christian role of the Oak King, amalgamating paganism with Christianity so perhaps the trees do contain both a language and a wisdom.

We were fools to cast it all away.

CHAPTER
SEVEN

The Company I Keep

'Twas an evening in November.
As I very well remember
I was walking down the street in drunken pride,
But my knees were all a flutter
So I landed in the gutter,
And a pig came up and lay down by my side.
Yes, I lay there in the gutter
Thinking thoughts I could not utter,
When a colleen passing by did softly say,
"Ye can tell a man that boozes
By the company he chooses," —
At that the pig got up and walked away.

Like that pig, I choose my company very carefully like my friend, who, as a man in his seventies could out-ride and out-hit my 16-year-old daughter in polo practice, said that at the age of five he had to decide whether he would choose to live with animals or humans . . . and chose the world of horses.

I had walked with the basset hound up the close-chewed grass of the downs, through the great flock of sheep whose eyes changed from vacancy to suspicion but with no apparent emotions in between, to the Sea Mark which has stood serene and useful on the highest point since the early eighteenth century, a stubby finger pointing to the eternity of the sky.

As a fixed point on the map it was used with the other fixed point, the white painted seaward wall of St Helen's Old Church (the new church, built so far inland as to be well outside the village, bears the arms of King George II) to accurately set compasses when they were "swung" by the great wooden-walled war ships, and that host of busy traders who imported Britain's wealth, in the great anchorage called Spithead. Britain dominated the world and the Sea Mark dominated the skyline.

I sprawled on my back on the turf and watched the clouds drift slowly by. The basset sat gazing contently into space with his dim eyes. Sheep wandered up and looked at him with lowered heads; he ignored them, but why, the day before had he behaved so strangely?

A gentle, elderly man in old fashioned bib-and-brace overalls had arrived with a canvas tool bag to fix the gas cooker with a flexible pipe, so that it could be wheeled out and cleaned beneath and behind.

The smallest child sat on the floor and passed the tools, usually the wrong ones, until the right one for the job could not be found.

"We'll need the big wrench from the van," the fitter said. "Let's go and look". Up jumped the smallest child, and taking him by the hand they walked through the house. The hound had watched the morning's work in silence, but the moment they moved he rushed past them and stood in the open front door growling and barking and refusing to allow them to pass . . . an Horatio on the bridge. And when a basset growls it is a sound as profound as Vesuvius working up a hate. But the moment the fitter dropped the hand of the smallest child the basset allowed him to pass.

How did he know? How could he have guessed that something might be amiss. We had never trained him to protect the children. What instinct suggested to him that the smallest child might be abducted?

In the deer park of a country house we had strolled ahead of the smallest child — she was still then in that different world where air-borne seeds were fairies and the whorls on the trunks of trees were hideous faces — when a barren red hind charged down on her, psychotic in the protection of her non-existent calf. The Basset galloped, his ears flying like miniature wings, and got himself between the child and the trampling hind.

With head held high he barked in that Cornetto di Basseto which says: "You shall not pass". And yet this behaviour was from an animal everyone described as congenitally the most stupid of hounds and therefore the dunce of the dog world.

There are usually simple explanations for animal behaviour — the scientific word for this study is ethnology — such as sight and sound, and some less easily explained to the lay person such as the echo-sounding used by bats or the use of light, the sun and the stars in both bird and animal migration — the sixth sense which humans appear to have lost. On our beach, almost a mile of flat, hard sand, we could attract the attention of leashed greyhounds, simply by waving white handkerchiefs. As you walked away into the distance they never for one moment took their eyes from the "flapper". They are not called "gazehounds" for nothing.

But could the Basset, inside a substantially built house, distinguish my car, as I changed down through the gears, from all the other rush hour cars during that time that I worked in town?

If you cut off your nose and opened it out flat the microscopic organs of the sense of smell would cover the area of a postage stamp while a dog has five times more, perhaps 250 million individual olefactory sensories in its nose. And yet we look down on animals as being inferior to humans. It is not the similarities between man and animals which attract me, but the ways our differences are used.

Men have, over the ages, put the extraordinary sensitivity of dogs' scenting ability to the test. Over 100 years ago twelve men, in a rather primitive experiment, set out on a long walk, each carefully treading in the exact footprint of the man in front. Eventually the group split up and each person walked off in a different direction. The leader's dog was then released and there are no prizes for guessing that it followed the trail faithfully until the point of dispersal where, without hesitation, it followed its master's scent.

But what happened when a dog was put through these paces with identical twins: at the point of dispersal, total confusion. Why not try these simple experiments yourself.

There is certainly nothing new about "second sight" or "the sixth sense" in animals. Some of them have solutions so simple that they are hardly worth wondering about.

In the 1830s one of the first of these simple observations was made in the town of Conception in Chile. Horses were seen to become agitated at 1.30 in the morning; all the dogs that could ran out of doors and an hour before that gulls had been seen in profusion, rising and unusually screaming into the air and at 11.40 . . . an earthquake destroyed the entire town.

That is all very well as it is easy to imagine that sensitive animals would repsond to distant tremors under the earth; you should see the speed earthworms can move at when a mole is burrowing nearby. But how does that account for precognition — the ability dogs and some other animals have to see into the future. A legion of stories from reliable sources and authenticated by independent witnesses concern dogs which have refused to leave a house, refused to get into a car, or have repeatedly and unusually hopped out of the back of a farm truck, and within the hour the car has crashed with death and injuries. There is even a well-authenticated case of a dog being loaded into a small open plane and repeatedly jumping out until it was left behind in exasperation. The plane crashed, killing the pilot and the dog's owner.

Equally often there is no logical or rational scientific explanation for animal behaviour. Then, by accident, you discover a so-far unrevealed secret and a chink of light shines into our understanding of animals.

For a lifetime I have known that if you want to tell a horse something you want it to remember you clasp your hands over its muzzle, breathe and talk into its nostrils while looking upwards into its eyes. Difficult that, because horses are herd animals of open prairies and steppes and the main, defensive range of their vision from the placing of the eyes is sideways with limited front vision.

So I adopted the habit of putting my arm under a horse's jaw, resting my head against its cheek so that the vibrations from my voice would carry through the bones of its head and so that I could look directly *sideways* into one eye.

Travelling up and down to watch polo at Cowdray Park I noticed a single grey gelding alone in a small paddock and used to stop to have a chat with the horse.

"Are you lonely?" I asked. When answering "yes" a horse "bridles", dips its head as if nodding in agreement.

"Would you like a friend?" The gelding bridled.

"Do you have a friend?" The gelding moved its head sideways as a human does when saying "no". Always keep the questions simple and allow the answers to build up into a complete picture, but in a thoughtless moment I asked a double negative: "You haven't got a friend, have you?" And to my surprise the horse turned its head sideways, not once but twice. It was able to answer a double negative with a double reply.

A few minutes later I tried another double negative question and the response was the same. It was no accident and I had learned something entirely new.

But you have to divide the company you keep between those which are close at hand, the farm animals and the domestic pets and geese, and those which you can see but can never touch, the wild swans and the whales and porpoises which abound around these coasts. I have an unexpressed feeling that many people who are close to wild life are both solitary by nature and romantics by instinct, or perhaps it is just that we see things in a different light.

In any case I should have guessed it was going to be one of those weekends . . . it was full of weird omens. First, I was in suit, collar and tie and heading towards a piano recital given by a young relative — he played Satie's "Gymnopédies" so I felt that I could forgive him the discomfort of the suit and tie.

As we were motoring through the side streets of the market town among the anonymous rows of red brick cottages, there was a peahen strutting elegantly along the pavement. She looked at us with a look which said: "You are the strangers in this town"; and strutted on unconcerned at our gawping.

It was a scene so bizarre I was reminded of that frightening scene when lions walked the streets of Rome before Ceasar was murdered and I pondered on the words of Calpurnia's tragic dream . . .

". . . Not heaven nor earth have been at peace this night."

The next morning we went to the cliff-edge to watch terns dive-bombing from fifty feet into a mirrored sea at what must have been a prodigious shoal of fish, if the excitement of the terns was anything to judge by. Then, as the morning warmed up we saw that vast numbers of swallows were riding the thermal contours over the sea as far to east and west as the binoculars would allow us to see.

Then, in the middle of all this movement and bustle of life we saw, at least half a mile offshore, swimming about as if it were the proprietor of all the Seven Seas, and in all its garish colours (with bright red knobs on!) a huge muscovy duck.

"Duck for dinner," Thomas said and stood at the furthest end of the breakwater shouting for the duck to come within snatching distance. The duck came quickly towards him and stayed just out of reach . . . no bread for me, no dinner for you was the message.

Then we saw something else, something strange and almost frightening in its strangeness in that calm sea. There was a plume of Herring gulls and Black-headed gulls, perhaps 200 or more of them, rising and falling on the water like a fountain of screaming agitation and, just under the surface of the clear water and over silvery sand, a slow moving, vast dark shadow drifting over the sea bed.

The whale, certainly twenty feet long, was browsing in the shallows with all the concern of a man pottering gently in his flower garden, oblivious of the world around him.

Why should I have been surprised? When I was a child I watched porpoises leaping through the tide race under Culver Cliff. What charmed me was that they seemed not only to enjoy this elaborate game but to share the fun with their companions. Lobster potting one day we caught that uncanny feeling that we were being watched. And we were.

Small, blue-grey faces were peering at us out of the water. They had come to see what we were doing in their ocean, attracted by the splashing of the pots and, across the surface of the water, our voices. I am sure that small whales — cetaceans — have acute hearing above water even if it is not as hypersensitive as when they are submerged. And like so many small whales they seemed to be smiling at us, their eyes glinting in merriment. They came slowly closer, watching us intently and then, as if replying to some unsaid word of command, they disappeared below the waves in an instant and we never saw them again.

In any year there are likely to be a hundred pilot whales similar to the one I saw and fifty killer whales, the black and white ones seen in so-called "Wildlife Parks", in the English Channel alone. The coastal waters of Britain have twenty-three recorded species of whales of which it is said that ten species are common and can be seen from beaches and tall cliffs. Add to this the huge numbers of smaller whales, the porpoises and dolphins and there are a thousand whales between Land's End and Dover.

But when you get into the warm waters of the Gulf Stream on the Atlantic coast of Ireland from the Aran Islands southwards, there may be 10,000 whales in the year. The larger stay off the Continental Shelf, while the smaller whales such as bottle-nosed dolphins and harbour porpoises congregate in vast herds chattering amongst themselves like excited children.

It is the sociability of whales which attracts us to them. Female porpoises with calves gather together in their own herds, rather like the sociable herds of mothers gathered at school gates to collect their children and to spread the news, myth and rumour of the village.

At sea, I am told by a Met man who served on Atlantic weather ships for many years, pilot whales almost thirty feet long would lie alongside all day carefully watching the weatherman at work. In the Antarctic my friend, Piglet, who served on a destroyer, a huge engine of war, which was acting as guardship when Sir Francis Chichester rounded the Horn, told me of whales rubbing their barnacle-encrusted backs on the ship's keel and the whole ship vibrating to their sensual pleasures. The prophet Jonah would have been impressed. That is what I call a real whale.

But do not make any mistake that these giants are only in distant waters. In the bleak years immediately after World War II when butcher's meat was at a premium, the then government set up a whaling industry in the Hebrides to cull those leviathans, the Blue Whales. The venture failed.

But whales are not the only creatures in the sea that are warm blooded, intelligent and inquisitive. Up in Orkney the sea was the tempting colour of liquid ice, the air as pure as light through a diamond and just as cold. No one was about. Slip off your clothes for the sheer exhilaration of a cold swim even if you can only stand three minutes of it. Four minutes will surely kill you.

In thirty seconds I was surrounded by friends with shining but furry faces and whiskers of clubland colonels, but with the sad and beautiful eyes that seals adopt when they find a lunatic trying to freeze himself to death in their particular patch of the sea.

At first I was tempted to apologise for my intrusion, but while we smiled at each other I suddenly thought about the narwhal, the one with the huge helical tusk which lives amongst the eskimo ice and was last accurately recorded in British waters in the 1920s, and laughed out loud at the thought that there are unicorns living under the sea . . .

All this illustrates the difference in relationships between man and animals and birds in isolation, and the companionship of animals. What intrigues is that every experience is different, differently understood, differently felt, differently explained but always enriching in triumph or disaster like a broken love affair which has a reward in the deeper understanding of the other person . . . or even yourself.

Some of my friends say: "I don't like horses, they frighten me". My experience, purely from observation, is that horses are frightened, certainly nervous, of people who are frightened of them and, without any doubt, can detect this fear at thirty yards or more, sometimes even on sight. We have often discussed this. Is it that our body temperature changes? Is it that minute movements which we do not notice are discernable to the horse? Do we perspire more? Certainly we underestimate both the visual ability of horses and their sense of smell.

Joe Royds, carrying a month-old grandchild, one of many, found the babe indifferent to him when wearing a "respectable" jacket. But once, when wearing a thoroughly disreputable stable jacket, the baby clung to the smelly coat showing pleasure and contentment. Now, Joe is not the sort of man who relies on one observation alone. The experiment was repeated and he publicly asked mothers if they had shared that experience. It, too, was no accident.

Was this another clue to that "unwritten" language between mentally handicapped, or those too immature to express themselves, and horses? Joe thinks so.

But it is the companionship of animals which provides the greatest pleasures: the idiosyncrasies of cats . . . a friend has two cats so different in personalities you would hardly believe they are the same species. One spends much of the day sitting behind a curtain on the window sill gazing out at a world in which very little happens. The other, when he is not asleep — cats spend about eighty per cent of their lives asleep — will, on command, leap on to the lady's bosom and throw his arms round her neck like a passionate lover and rest his head against her. Then he allows himself to be carried about the house in this odd way.

Our farm cats were fat as pigs. We never fed them. They were on the payroll and had to earn their keep. Watching Nicholas, a black Tom with a white bib of just such a size that he looked like a boulevardier prowling off to dinner in a smart restaurant, walking through wet grass reduced us to helpless laughter. He delicately placed each foot in the grass as if he were walking on Skylarks' eggs. Then he raised a foot and shook the water off like an old man shaking a wet umbrella. When there were mice in the corn bin he was popped in to deal with the rogues. He sat there looking around unable to see them.

"He needs a pair of specs," the cowman said, "and he's daft enought to wear them."

Cats are the strangest delusion of self-satisfaction: as in the case of the little grey-haired lady sitting contentedly by the fireside with her pet cat for companionship. As a vision it is, of course, quite wrong.

The truth is that the elderly, those of sixty-five years and older, own fewer cats than any other section of the community. Young, middle class families with small children are the people who own cats and most other pets.

These two facts are pointers to what is a continuing and increasing social disgrace. Most of us long ago discarded the idea that, except for a small minority of devotedly responsible people, we are the world's pre-eminent nation of pet lovers even though the great majority of the five million plus dogs and almost five million pet cats are owned by people who care for their pets, value their unique companionship and feel a deep sense of bereavement when they die. But in any year the RSPCA has to take charge of 100,000 dogs of which over 50,000 have to be killed because they are too sick, or injured, too old or simply because it is not possible to find homes for them.

To anyone who has only two dogs or a pair of cats the idea of 50,000 is beyond imagination ... and the RSPCA points out that it is an animal welfare organisation not an agency for the destruction of animals.

113

The truth about strays is that they are the puppies which made the mistake of growing up. What was once a bundle of furry fun quickly became a great hungry creature which required endless exercise.

That Christmas kitten also creates his own problems, tearing at the furniture and curtains before entering into an operatic career serenading his lady loves in the lee of the compost heap at night.

Nothing ever stays the same for long and the patterns of pet ownership are always changing, but cat ownership amongst the elderly will probably stay the same for the next twenty five years largely because the number of elderly people will remain static during that time. One of the most interesting facts in the often lonely world of the elderly, many of whom have lost a husband or a wife, is that when the cat dies they refuse to get another, even a give-away, because they cannot stand the grief of losing another partner, or do not themselves want to die and leave their cat in a friendless world. Incidentally, about ninety-five per cent of all people over sixty-five still live at home.

If there is going to be any change in pet ownership it is likely to be amongst the traditional pet-owning salaried middle classes who suffer from every frost and thaw in the economic climate. They are the ones who have to budget whether they can keep the family car on the road *and* have a foreign holiday each year, but can they then afford the reasonable cost of boarding the dog or cat? Emotion is a powerful persuader, but the bank manager's sword is sharp and that Christmas puppy becomes this year's summer stray. Sadly, heart-breakingly sadly, those stories about dogs being pitched out of cars on the motorways are true.

My friend Kenneth Christopherson, who insures people's pets, sees even greater social significance in pet ownership and believes that many fathers buy, ostensibly for their children, large dogs because they are an expression of vicarious masculinity — "Look at me, I am wearing a great big fierce dog today". It is an extension of the statistically proven fact that drivers of red cars are more frequently involved in accidents than people in green cars. Kenneth also points out that while some small dogs are bought by women as surrogate children, many more are bought for the same reason that they wish to be admired for wearing ornamental jewellery . . . And you thought they were just cats and dogs?

If anything, the plight of many pet horses is worse than that of many "indoor" pets. Pet horses, and there are probably half a million of them, can be seen on the fringes of many towns, even the small ones, where tiny paddocks are often populated by cheap, ill-bred and run-down ponies suffering from the inexperience, ignorance and lack of spare spending money of their owners. I have seen horses kept in back gardens, garages and in one case in the disused coal-store of a pub.

But these are not the only pressures on pet ownership: almost forty per cent of local authorities have restrictions against keeping cats, although few enforce them on the six million people who live in council owned property. And please do not think this is an urban problem because rural authorities have even greater powers over the keeping of hens and other domestic-cum-farm animals. And while governments have been energetically lobbied to control stray dogs it is unlikely to introduce legislation to control cats because they have an image of being clean, causing no damage and being affectionate, when there is no zoological evidence to support any of these received images.

Add to this the unwelcome fact that almost one third of all elderly people suffer from a mental or physical infirmity and that many do not receive visits from neighbours, relatives or friends. This makes the ownership of a pet, any pet, vitally important not only for companionship but also for constancy in an ever-changing world.

And yet amongst those elderly people who do not own a cat, there is no expressed intention of ever getting one and anyone can understand that those who have experienced bereavement will feel the loss of an animal with almost the same emotional intensity as that of a human companion.

There are also the other sorts of pet — the comedians.

You would have thought the great pagan god Bacchus had returned to earth; he stands broadly there with curled hair and grizzled beard, his arms and face leathered deep brown with constant exposure to the country air and sun. He "farms" eighteen acres of downland vines on land not unlike the rolling chalk hills of champagne country at Rheims and Epernay. This is a very large acreage compared to many of the famous

116

French vineyards. His job is to tend the vines and produce the grapes; others make the wine. His companion in the many solitary hours of working this yard is a chocolate-coloured Field Spaniel. With his large feet, pointed crown and feathered legs he is something of a half-wit. Perhaps he wins prizes at country fairs for his lack of gumption.

The vines run in military precision up the sides of the downs. They are the conventional Muller-Thurgau; but there are also plastic tunnels where the viticulturist is playing with a Pinot noir grape — the great fat red grape which makes white champagne — some hybrid German vines so new that they have no name and even, experimentally, vines from Siberia.

The Romans grew vines north of the Tyne, but this modern Bacchus believes there has been a fundamental change in the British climate — there is plenty of rural evidence to support this view — over the centuries. One year Adgestone made 65,000 bottles of wine . . . the next only 8,000, then 70,000. You do not need to have the risks or the vagaries of the weather explained to you. But when you discover that this vineyard exports to France and California and produces a favoured drink amongst the princelings of the Rhine, you realise how good the product must be. Vintners from near Perigord, where the summer temperature peaks 100°F, come to Adgestone to marvel that wine can be made so far north.

But there are four uncultivated acres next to the vines waiting to be planted, and although the vineyard is fenced against ever-nibbling rabbits a family of hares is in residence: we believe they have a secret postern gate and despite everything they are safer here than on the barley stubbles higher up the down where an aircraft sprayed the weeds and a few days later the carcasses of a dozen hares were found.

And while we sample the vintage in the deep cold caves the loopy dog plays elaborate games. In that field, which in summer is as rich with flowers as an alpine meadow, he searches out the hares and chases them.

It is a job for which he is totally unsuited.

The hares run a couple of hundred yards at what appears to be the speed of light, their ears folded down their backs; then they stop, stand almost upright and look at the spaniel in exasperation. It is that look of exasperation which says: "I don't want to play your game."

Toby hunts up hill, nose to ground towards the hare which promptly gallops back, missing the dog by only a yard or so, to the exact place from which he started. The dog is utterly confused and hunts carefully back down the hill and so the game continues.

Then there is his Keystone Kops routine: the vineyard is encircled with windbreak poplars; with Grey alders between the vines and Italian alders across the lines. These are planted not only as windbreaks but because the leaves retain the heat of the sun even after it has set and it is warmth rather than direct sunlight that ripens grapes . . .

Suddenly the hare rockets out of the crossbreaks inches from the spaniel's brown-button nose, then recrosses the line at another junction in what must be an inevitable ninety degree collision just like the Kops and the speeding tramcar in the old films. Naturally they miss each other by only millimetres. The game goes on until the dog is exhausted and he drinks from the muddy puddle where the tap constantly drips and then falls asleep in the shade under the vines. The hare, a few yards away, sits and watches over him at sleep.

The next illusion is played late autumn at dawn and dusk and is called bird-scaring. Bacchus fires a 12-bore cartridge high over the perimeter poplars where dagger-beaked starlings and loose flocks of mistle thrushes gathering up in preparation for the winter are waiting to pounce in their hundreds on the ripening grapes — picking in this vineyard goes on into November. But that was no ordinary cartridge. There is a vivid white flash and a huge explosion in the air but never any casualties.

But the dog, despite the fact that he has never been trained to retrieve, thinks he is out rough shooting and sets off to collect birds which are already squawking alive in the next village.

So far Toby has not caught a hare or any of the partridges which live in the grass, or retrieved a starling (unless one dies of shock) and, frankly, I will give you odds of a thousand to one that he never will.

Hare populations are a constant mystery; in one rural county not a hare to be seen, a few miles away hares beyond count. While walking unobserved across deep plough above Arreton I saw forty hares on one meadow sparring and dashing about in wild and frantic circles like the proverbial Mad March Hare . . . except that it was February.

Eventually we emerge from our tasting in those chilly cellars and climb into bright and bewildering sunlight. The dog long ago gave up his hopeless game and is lying in the shade of the vines and we discover that the smallest child has found a leveret crouching in the grass.

She is sitting amongst the early flowers and is cuddling the leveret up close in her arms while it rests patiently and motionless, its ears laid back, its eyes wide open.

"What are you doing?" I ask.

"I'm telling this little hare a story," the smallest child says.

There is no answer to that. It is the company she keeps.

CHAPTER
EIGHT

A One Way Pendulum?

I am not a doomwatcher. I do not believe in the ultimate downfall of man or of the birds and animals which surround him; the millions of plants, too few of which I know; the uncounted millions of insects which some doomwatchers insist will inherit the earth after a nuclear holocaust (if there is to be a holocaust it is already here and it is called man, he is the most destructive element in the history of time); or the fishes in the silent and secret world beneath the waves.

But, to paraphrase, the price of beauty is eternal vigilance otherwise the "Birds of the air *will* come a-crying and a-sobbing". How long will it be before we appreciate the true extent of the disaster of the vast, ruinously expensive, unwanted and wholly destructive effect of the post-war motorway systems of Europe and north America. How long will it be before we get the priorities of animal conservation right? Every year organised coursing with greyhounds kills about 1,000 brown hares. In each year between 600,000 and one million hares are killed on the roads of Britain. There is agitation and even violence to ban hare coursing, but there is no similar campaign to fence motorways against the indiscrimate killing not only of the possible million hares, but also foxes by the tens of thousand, badgers, countless stoats and weasels, magpies and crows . . .

Fortunately the pendulum of time and the constant changes in climate are always at work and often at work in our favour. We would all do well for ourselves if we read and interpreted the clues correctly.

The indicators have been easy to see over the last hundred or so years: the colonisation of Britain by the Scandinavian goosander; the toe-hold in south east England of the Cetti's warbler; the minute extension of the range of the Avocet (largely due to the draining of the Zuider Zee) into East Anglia; the widespread distribution of the groaning Collared dove, commonly and wrongly known in my childhood as the "Egyptian" dove.

Then there is the direct intervention of man, small and puny by comparison with the brute force of nature; the equation of the re-introduction of the capercaillie into Scotland plus the re-afforestation of vast tracts of moorland with conifers which has allowed the "old man of the forest" to drift slowly southwards. The gradual enlargement of the range of the Golden eagle is a direct result of legislative protection (and more enlightened land management amongst the highland lairds), while some catch-all enactments such as the Wildlife and Countryside Act have been quickly exposed as utterly ineffective and in some cases, such as the protection of Sites of Special Scientific Interest, actually damaging the legitimate protection and preservation of some species, especially the "hawk" families. And then, as we were taking our well-earned pint in the pub one Sunday lunchtime — at least, I like to believe it was well-earned — my fisherman friend said that in his opinion the autumns were getting warmer and the springs cooler. The man who is there and sees and touches is the man who knows and he is now catching lobsters until late into November, unheard of even ten years ago ... and strange exotic crabs which look as if they have wandered out of the tropics are now being caught in his pots.

I had already noticed that gold-crested wrens appear to be over-wintering south of the Thames. In order to understand how the pendulum is swinging and that it swings forward as well as backwards is to look northwards, if not into the arctic then to an area where the occasional icy finger of the arctic prods at wildlife, into Scotland and the more remote of the northern isles. But first of all let us try to get a couple of perspectives of what I am talking about in the area of change.

In the early 1950s the viral disease myxomatosis arrived in Britain, whether it was callously introduced by human agency or not is still, and is unlikely to ever be, resolved. But the collapse of the rabbit population had widespread repercussions throughout the animal and bird world.

But the pendulum swung back, if not nationally, then certainly in significant patches. Thirty years later we stood in a valley on Exmoor and clapped our hands. Suddenly the earth and grass around us seemed as if it were infected with a vast grey skin disease. The rabbit was back in business ... and in a very big way.

If I had heeded the obvious clue I might have guessed. Above us, high in the sky, was a mewing buzzard, and rabbit is an important part of its diet.

In my wildlife travels at that time, from the north Yorkshire moors, the Yorkshire dales, the Derbyshire Peaks, to Exmoor, the Isle of Wight and Sussex, I was able to confirm that the rabbit is not only back in business but in places in plague proportions, and with no indication so far of the myxomatosis which previously decimated them. The popular belief is that rabbits have both developed natural resistance to the disease and the habit of no longer living below ground except to give birth.

Whatever the truth of that I can tell you that on the Cowdray estate at Midhurst £10,000 was spent in one year on rabbit fencing; the rabbits in the embankment of the old Petworth to Midhurst railway have been digging up the hallowed Ambersham polo ground; new beech plantings at Watership Down in Hampshire have, ironically, had to be protected from rabbits, and the annual damage to forestry, horticulture and agriculture is estimated at £ 100 million a year at the very least.

But is this entirely bad news? Probably not. Over the centuries the rabbit established itself as a basic food source for a large number of indigenous species of birds and animals . . . the rabbit is as much an influence on the southward spread of the Wild cat and the Golden eagle as forest.

Not in over twenty years have I seen so many stoats and weasels in southern England, nor in such magnificent pelage or such good health, their russet coats looking as if they were newly painted and burnished. In ground ivy by a public footpath I watched a weasel stalking a young rabbit and standing upright every foot or so to peer round the terrain. I have even been surprised at the number of stoats and weasels on the fringe of London's suburbia.

No fools those stoats. A doe rabbit will easily have half a dozen litters a year between January and June, each gestation taking only four weeks and the doe ready to mate again within twelve hours of parturition. The rabbit has the fastest food to body weight conversion of any British wild, or domestic, animal and as a small hint to weight-watchers, they have no inter-muscular fat and are therefore valuable to those on a diet.

And so the pendulum swings: the westward drift of the buzzard to the Isle of Wight was only halted with the introduction of "myxie" but now I have seen an immature female Buzzard working the cliffs near Shanklin. If the rabbit is re-established in large numbers it is possible that there will be extensive wildlife benefits. In hard weather otters, decimated throughout much of Britain by dieldrin, will take rabbits; badgers are particularly fond of young rabbits and will dig furiously for them; but, then, badgers will dig for the sheer fun of it and rabbits are the staple diet of rural foxes.

There is now little doubt in my mind that the collapse of the rabbit population stimulated fox colonisation of city centres where food was, and still is, plentiful and territories largely undisputed. The only question which now requires an answer is what effect the rabbit explosion will have on rural foxes. Since 1945 the population of rural foxes has been gently but continuously rising. In a year foxhunters may kill up to 20,000 foxes, no one knows the total which I have heard sensible foxhunters quote at only half my figure. Many of these foxes are hunted as known and identified killers of farm or domestic livestock. In many of the Fell counties foxes are hunted on foot "by appointment" and having seen the vile damage a vixen can cause to a flock of new-dropped lambs I can assure you that some foxy accounts are overdue. Add to this, casual shooting and indiscriminate trapping (much now taken over in urban and suburban areas by local authorities), and at least the same number are killed.

But now, well fed on high protein food, it is possible that while there is a finite number for urban foxes based on the availability of food and territory, the rural fox population may peak to new highs.

I do not hunt, except out of curiosity but I hope that foxhunters will cope intelligently with this new situation. The fox has no natural predators although I estimate that the "spring kill" of young foxes on Britain's motorways is between 60,000 and 100,000 each year, but in nature animals to a quite large extent exist by the stimulation of predation and every species, almost without exception, has evolved physiological responses, however imperfect, to this stimulation.

The strange paradox to all this is "the Danish experience"; there is no fox hunting in Denmark after the British pattern so foxes are controlled by shooting. A wholly reliable scientific survey over a period of many years showed that where foxes were shot their numbers consistantly increased to meet the level of predation by humans. Hunting, as opposed to trapping, gassing or shooting (which is not done on a sufficiently large scale to effect fox populations in Britain) is the only extension by man to create natural predation.

But it is not only amongst animals that the hand of man may create situations of which there may be unpredictable consequences.

There was cold — iron cold and relentless. The wind was through the eye of the compass. I stood on a beach near the mouth of Wootton Creek in a February gale.

Suddenly, out of that grey seascape where grey sky melded into a grey sea obliterating all sense of distance and direction and where no sun shone, a skein of about forty Brent geese hurtled down the gale, spun in a majestic arabesque at the mouth of the creek and settled inside a shingle bank, preening, stretching their wings before settling and chattering amongst themselves like forty old biddies at a village whist drive.

Brent's are perhaps — there is plenty of competition — the ultimate paradox of survival and conservation in which we British can take some modest pride.

It is said that as far back as Kubla Khan, he of the "stately pleasure domes" and "twice five miles of fertile ground with walls and towers girdled round", put down millet and other hard grains for Partridge and Quail although I have a feeling that he was probably more interested in shooting the game than conserving them. But it does show that there is nothing new in the principles of conservation, not since the eleventh century, that is.

Yet until recent history, even in post war Britain, wildfowl have been regarded as a surplus crop. There were so many of them, so often and so predictable.

As a child I watched vast planks of duck ride a force nine off Bembridge Ledge. What were they? How many? One day a Smew, the smallest of the mergansers and one of the most beautiful birds in Europe, was washed ashore and I drew countless pencil lines of its singular beauty.

Not any more, they are far too common. Except for the traditional breeding grounds, many species of duck and geese have made a subtle change from natural habitats to managed lands. Many of the fifty-five species of European wildfowl, especially the browsers — those that walk our fields — have established an almost symbiotic relationship with man. Despite the fact that up to seventy per cent of many species are killed at the nest by arctic foxes and voracious gulls, and despite the skills of British wildfowlers, the populations of most species are increasing and some of these populations are causing concern — a goose may eat one third of its body weight each day from profitable crops. The needs of flying demand that geese cannot store food in their bodies ... in the short Icelandic summer a gosling needs to feed for twenty hours a day to gain sufficient strength for winter migration. Brents, wintering in northern Russia and Siberia, fly 3,000 miles to my beach.

This once threatened species now graze amongst the seaweed on our beach. They regard our spaniel with dismal contempt and you almost have to step over them. They certainly won't hurry to get out of your way. It seems that they are more than aware that they are one hundred and one per cent protected by law even though their population is constantly growing.

At one time it was said that Brent geese could only survive on eel grass (*Zostera*). Ask a few farmers in Essex or Hampshire if that is still true and you will get an hour-long lecture on the morality of the over-protection of geese.

But I lie in bed at dawn listening to Canada geese, a rarity in my youth, gossiping and cronking as they fly down in ragged V-skeins to fresh water drinking. How many ducks and geese and swans are we talking about? The mute swan, to me one of the most spectacular and romantic birds in flight, numbers 15,000 plus in Britain; 20,000 plus in the Netherlands and over 90,000 wintering birds in Denmark; so that the three countries contain almost all of the world's population, and it is not, in wildlife terms, a very big population.

The Spitzbergen population of Pink-foot geese is only 12,000 pairs with another 10,000 in Iceland and in scattered communities in Greenland. Most of them come to Britain to trespass on our fields in winter. The migratory Shoveller duck amounts to only about 20,000 on the continent.

But for all the problems facing this relationship, and the challenge it presents to us to cope with the swing of this particular pendulum, the magic and mystery of geese will continue to puzzle and haunt us watchers in the dawn. Why do Greenland and Spitzbergen Barnacle geese come to England and the Russian barnacles to the Netherlands, and with practically no swopping of locale? Why do 100,000 Shelduck congregate in one small area of the Heligoland Bight? Will the draining of the Somerset Levels near Bridgwater drive away this spectacular bird? Why, even, is Britain winter host to half the world's Shelduck population?

I moved on to Newtown Creek and sat under the old sea wall. Grey plovers stood about on the mud like glittering pearls and like myself tried to escape the bitter fingers of that criminal wind. Shelduck, as bright as painted parrots, battered down the gale onto the open mud flats where they stood about as garish as tarts at a garden party in the more sedate company of curlew, whimbrel and redshank. And although it was cold, bitterly bleak and friendless . . . I was happy.

There is a curious idea fixed in the minds of so many people, possibly those who do not have regular access to the countryside and the coast or do not live in our rural isolation, that nothing ever changes. Well, we have seen from these few examples that everything is changing . . . constantly. But there are some things in our world which do not change, which become tokens of stability rather like aristocratic families which pass on their titles from one generation to the next as the heads of the family fade away.

I have friends like this. Let me put it this way: there are badgers in East Woods. Nothing new about that, I

130

hear you say. The badgers have been in residence in East Woods for the thick end of 300 years. The evidence is clear before your eyes.

The bank stretches for some fifty yards, facing north and some degree west, at least twelve feet high at one end and drifting with the contour of the wood to a few feet at the other. It makes no difference. The whole is pierced with the entrances and exits of the badgers' many chambered setts.

I stand twenty yards back in the calm of the evening in full knowledge that I have been walking gingerly on someone's drawing room ceiling. This wood is masked in silence and gently washed with the soft gold of the last of the day's sun. The two old dears who planted it a lifetime and a half ago knew more than a hatful about planting trees. They planted this knife-edged ridge because it was too steep for grazing; they put two lines of cherry and two lines of sweet chestnut around the perimeter — in their day every estate made its own chestnut fencing — then they put yew and holly, probably for furniture making by further generations but which now call the pigeons in to roost from the cold plough. And right at the highest point, visible from their now decaying mansion, they planted limes and beech to provide an autumn crown of gold at the highest point of the East Woods.

But they left the badgers when they cleared the primeval scrub and planted the woods.

At the entrance to the sett, where vast amounts of scurry are churned out almost daily, you can find the bones and skulls of long-dead badgers.

I know it to be true that badgers die in the labyrinths below and are dragged into burial chambers and the entrances "bricked up" until, many years later, they are disinterred — why, nobody knows — and the white bones of forgotten ancestors are scattered amongst the smooth-boled beeches down the escarpment.

On odd days, and there appears to be no reason for this, although I liken it to a woman's inescapable urge to re-arrange the furniture in the drawing room, their entire bedding will be scattered outside their myriad front doors. Twigs, leaves, straws, an ocean of bracken and all the garbage of an acquisitive animal are all cast out in brilliant sunshine to be sniffed over and then dragged back into the halls and chambers where entire families live, including that goodly collection of "nippers" that scrapped amongst the leaves with parents, uncles, aunts, grand-parents and an unaccountable legion of maiden ladies.

They sniff at the air, the nose held high, twisting and twizzling. The sharp, dark eyes are taking in the world into which, unforgiven, I have encroached. There is no secret about badger watching. You must be down wind and you must be silent. The slightest smell of human will drive them back below so will the slightest movement or unnatural cracking of a twig or stirring of a history of dead leaves.

I stand with my back to a heavy tree with a five foot thumb stick to lean forward on. In this pose I can stand for hours until darkness overwhelms me. One evening a small flock of longtailed tits came into one of those evergreen thorns which crackle and spit when thrown onto a fire. I was standing so quiet and still I was convinced they would perch on my shoulders. I suppose I meld easily into this treescape. I have rubbed my hands with earth and leaves to disguise my scent. I came from the earth; I smell of the earth. My friends live under the earth.

Watching the badgers, I have no doubts about their country myths: there are plenty of authenticated stories of badger cubs which have died near setts being carefully covered with leaves and dried grass. But equally, there are as many stories where known parents have ignored the carcasses of their dead children. I also know of many authenticated stories of badgers hauling traffic injured relatives off roadways.

I lie in that bed, from which I hear the geese, under windows which have been left open so long they have rusted into position. Once, in order to hear the sounds of night better, I moved the bed right under the open window and was woken in the grey hour before dawn soaking wet where the rain had driven through the window. You can take your enthusiasms too far, you know. But the compensation is that I can hear every movement outside and I am so attuned to night that I can identify the hedgehogs gardening for me. Suddenly my skin creeps when I hear a wandering badger scream for territory or in the hope of hearing an answering scream. That and the screech of a vixen calling for a lover are the two most chilling sounds in the British countryside.

When the badger cubs are sufficently grown they are unceremoniously kicked out of house and home. It is a noisy affair with much snapping and growling, pushing and shoving, but never with wounds or injuries. They must find a wife of their own; find their own home, even if it is already part tenanted by other badgers, because badgers will accept a newcomer into their setts to strengthen the blood of the family.

And while they are wandering they come battling through my garden; my fences and hedges are no defence to a badger seeking a new home. You can put up string dipped in creosote, you can lock up your hens, but a hungry badger knows more than a hundred tricks of how to get into a hen house. Unfortunately they sometimes forget the good manners of the table and gorge themselves and fall asleep at the scene of the crime . . . punishment can be dire.

But up in the East Wood we are alone. There is no time here; there is no place. The badgers conduct their rituals in the same precise details that they have conducted them for many hundreds of years. They know that we are only tenants in time and space. Before creeping away in the darkness I bow my head to my friends. They bow back; to them ritual and ceremony is all.

That is why I shall not tell you exactly where the East Wood lies.

Having seen the extreme of mobility and movement and how some animals such as urban foxes have responded to the influence of man while others, my badger friends in particular, hardly seem to change over the centuries, we can look back again at the climate and its profound effect on man and the animals and birds which surround him.

In the history of time it is only a minute ago that wild ox and boar roamed the English countryside. Even animals as familiar as Fallow deer have two distinct occupations of Britain. As the ice-cap of the last great ice age crept southwards so the deer fled across the river which separated us from Europe . . . Fallow deer are still referred to as a "Mediterranean" species but when the ice melted they forgot to come back and had to be re-introduced by the Phoenicians, by the Romans, who now knows?

It is easy to understand the massive influence a climate change of many thousands of years may have on a landscape and overlook the equally dramatic changes which can occur in a single lifetime. The doomwatchers point out the constant erosion of the countryside as tens of thousands of acres are mangled for new roads, industrial estates and housing. And yet, in the last 100 odd years more different species of birds — about 200 are breeding, the litmus test of birds' presence — are found in Britain than ever before, among which about 170 nest in Scotland. Most of these are new nesters and are unfamiliar to any but the most committed bird watcher — even a keen amateur such as myself has problems with the Red necked phalarope (the clue to this bird is Women's Lib; the rather dowdy little male incubates the eggs while the more colourful females forage for food), Temminck's stint or the Green sandpiper which does a sort of cuckoo by taking over the abandoned homes of tree nesting birds.

All these birds and others are post war arrivals — the massive Snowy owl which settled on the remote island

135

of Fetlar; the Red throated diver; and the still very rare Great northern diver whose blood curdling calls will chill your whole body as it swims on the remote sea lochs of The Isles. The Americans, perhaps more accurately call this bird the Loon ... but no human, insane or otherwise, could make such an unearthly call.

Add to this some of the more spectacular species of arctic duck: the Scaup, whose filigree-marked feathers are worth an hour of anyone's study, the sea-going Scoter and the odd but rapid southern spread of the Eider, the one which uses its own feathers in profusion to line its nest in the rocks and pebbles of Iceland, and from which the original eiderdowns were made. The best place to see them today is in their colony on the Farne Islands off the Northumberland coast where they are surprisingly tame. But now these arctic ducks have even colonised parts of the Mediterranean.

Perhaps part of this influence on wildlife is in the very slight change, and it has only to be very slight to have a fundamental effect on animal behaviour, in wind direction with slightly fewer westerly winds in spring and autumn — although the number of rare vagrants buffeted here from America and continental Europe on the gales does not seem to have declined. But the increased north and south winds have carried the common birds of Iceland, Finland and the great windswept tundras to us, while our common and seemingly fragile garden birds such as warblers and chaffinches have drifted northwards. At one time Bramblings, like overweight and over-painted chaffinches, were rarely seen in the south with winter flocks of chaffinches in our garden. Now they are certainly not common, but equally, they are not unusual.

There are cautions to be made: in my childhood Yellowhammers and Hawfinches, especially in winter flocks, were common. Now, this is not so. But they are not uncommon in neighbouring counties. We must not judge simply on what occurs on our own cabbage patch. The second caution concerns that ubiquitous animal, the "Twitcher", with his strange plumage, telescopes, tripods, notebooks and maps. This is the headlong birdwatching enthusiast who sometimes collects bird sightings as small boys collect train numbers. Their records, forever adding to the British list of sightings, may be in a strict proportion to the number of Twitchers available on the ground at any one time and often suggests that the birds were there all the time but no-one noticed or bothered to make an official record.

The final caution is illustrated by the Osprey which returned as a nesting species to Strathspey in Scotland, after decades of wrongful persecution, post war. Was this the influence of man through protective legislative, climatic change or simply that these birds, filling the niche between the White-tailed sea eagle, recently reintroduced from Norway to the island of Rhum to breed and recolonise Scotland, and the indigenous Golden eagle, merely re-occupied the northern fringe of their existing nesting range?

Nothing changes — everything changes. The arm of the pendulum swings backwards and forwards . . . and the clock ticks relentlessly on.

CHAPTER NINE

Time Out of Mind

A hundred years ago this village hardly existed. Queen Victoria lived a dozen miles away in her ornate Italianate summer house overlooking the hermaphrodites of steam and sail which clustered in the Solent and Spithead. She had come a long way since, as an excitable girl new to the throne, she had giggled and chattered nervously on the steep hill at Ryde where her hotel is now holiday flats.

Her courtiers built vast and usually ugly miniature palaces along the beaches, but they might have been on the dark side of the moon as far as this village was concerned. Here there was a scattering of cottages, some hardly more than huts, a row or two of more substantial houses in red brick made from the spoils of profitable smuggling, in those days a sophisticated and respected trade, all at arm's length from the farms and half a world away from the great manor house.

Between times the monarchs have come and gone, the titled and bemedalled courtiers and their jewelled ladies have become footnotes in history books for those who care to look for them. But our history is written in the land.

Reading title deeds to land sold in the 1860s for "new" development, I saw that the original field in which the house I was interested in buying was named "Pigge's Bottom". A "Bottom" is just that; the lower edge of a steep decline, usually wooded and often where the spread of woodland is limited by a stream or swampy ground. But who or what was named for "Pug's Hole"? Who was the "Steppe" of "Steppe's Mesh" (a mesh is a marsh) and who was the Brook, a common enough name around here, after whom "Brook's Furlong" was named, corrupted into "Brook's Verland" in local dialect or one vurle or furrow's length in ploughing.

Every field, every parcel of land, even "No Man's"; every copse, every spinney and sometimes even ditches and thick ancient hedges had names. And as you can date the antiquity of a hedge by the number of species of tree growing in it, or the possible dates of bridle roads from villages long since disappeared — I defy anyone to walk through Glover's or down to St Urian's which the French destroyed in the 1540s without being overwhelmed with that deep sense of brooding which comes from loitering with time out of mind — so you can date the fields themselves. The names are the embodiment of our history; they mean a lot to us. But not to everyone.

There was a plot of building land next to a small range of stables on the edge of the village. An elderly couple from a distant county bought the plot, built a bungalow on it and promptly retired into it.

A few weeks later they complained to the local authority that the air was full of the smell of horses and the unwelcome odours of the dung heap, the clanking of horses in the early morning and the bustle of tacking-up.

In a few months the stables were closed on the grounds of nuisance it caused the local residents.

Others also complained about the smell of silage, the heavy stench of slurry spread on the fields and mud on the roads, even though it was correctly signposted with warnings and swept up afterwards. They complained about the smell of rotting seaweed strewn along a mile of beach . . . "Why doesn't the council do something about it?" they asked.

We might be forgiven for thinking that those who retire to the countryside do so to participate in it. But is that true?

Take another example: that stone-built cottage with the lichened roof and roses round the door, which stands below the downs, costs £10,000 more to buy than a village house because its picturesqueness can be bought with the accumulated wealth of matured insurance polices and a lifetime of prudent savings from salaried income plus a substantial company pension. The cowman and the shepherd, meanwhile, live in council houses.

But the retired couples who buy these homes are far from their families; there are only two buses a day, one each way, to the supermarket, the village shop is by necessity more expensive, and they do not supplement their larders from the gardens which were devised to keep a man, his wife and three children in root and green vegetables and soft fruits for at least nine months a year. By the way, the lane is muddy where the cows

140

amble down from the high fields, it is unlit and overhung with brambles and does not have the security of a pavement in the dark.

The retired couples have not bought the serenity and security of their urban dreams but, too often, increasing worry and self-imposed hardship which pride rarely allows them to admit. Even their gardens outgrow their declining strength and they become, too often, prisoners in rural isolation. Never is there a better example of this than in those infrequent years when snow brings everything except the farming community to a halt.

To those used to suburban convenience and the high requirements of that way of life there is the question: how do you adapt your life to an older property? A flagged floor is very pretty and cold; a broad oak floor holds the dirt and is draughty; doors and windows do not fit — a cottage I looked at had the original door fittings, one latch, no lock, and window glass from the day it was built in the 1740s — the flames from the fire roar up the chimney to warm the stars. The bread oven has been bricked up or been opened out to display the family geraniums and African violets and yet it was intended, and works very efficiently, as the house's central heating system, usually running between the cottage's two principal rooms and sometimes with dampers to control heating to upper rooms.

Cast iron stoves, stoutly fire-blacked, were torn out years ago when town gas arrived in the countryside. These stoves were temperamental, dirty and probably the most efficient piece of domestic cottage equipment invented; multi-purpose and economical. Today I find even the draught holes in front of open fires blocked, but it does not matter, there is a mono-purpose, high energy, high cost gas or electric fire in the hearth now. Worse, central heating is installed and centuries of woodwork shrinks and splits.

What appears to be happening is that inexperienced cottage owners are trying to adapt old houses to their received expectancies, the romantic view of country life, when it is easier for humans to adapt themselves to the natural limitations of the houses as they were originally built. In order to live successfully in an Elizabethan house you have to go through the difficult metamorphosis of thinking as an Elizabethan. But it takes courage to discard a lifetime of ideas and the accepted comforts of life; it is also difficult to discard unused and unusable furniture, to tolerate the discomfort of cold and wet. Two hundred years ago you would have been hard pressed to find a dozen pieces of substantial furniture in a cottage. They were not needed. What was important was that garden, which today contains lawns and flowers, not energy; a supply of wood, a brew house and a cold room.

The truth is simple if you can accept it: it is more difficult to live in the countryside than it is to live in a town. It is more demanding of intelligence and ingenuity and physical strength than suburban life, and while it is possible to change some aspects to raise the quality of country life to the expectations created by glossy magazine thinking, it is not possible to make enough changes, without fundamentally changing the whole fabric of life, for rural life to conform to suburban dreams of rurality.

High disposable margins of income now allow couples to live in houses devised for complete families: Jacobean manor houses built for two families and half a dozen servants now house one elderly couple; no wonder they complain about the running expenses and the cold. The great houses, in their eighteenth-century glory may have contained over a hundred people under one roof, they were designed for over a hundred people and built to sustain such numbers and even today they have not worn out while streets of cottages and jerry-built "spec" houses from the 1920s are fading away.

Within this discussion lies one of the great politicised myths of the twentieth century: that domestic service was a form of slavery at worst and abject servitude at best. This may well have been true of pretentious lower middle class houses in late Victorian years but most of the evidence, and there is no shortage of it, of life in the great houses in the classic period of British house building between roughly 1650 and 1850 suggests that domestic service was at the pinnacle of sought-after jobs in rural Britain.

Remember that not all country cottages were stone and thatch. Many of the transient homes of outside workers such as woodlanders, bodgers and shepherds were temporary hovels. Many cottages were damp beyond today's belief; farm wages were minuscule with long hours, few days of rest, inadequate clothing and few prospects. The great houses offered not only full time employment, but dry rooms and beds, at least one suit of clothes a year with boots or shoes, three meals a day in the servants' hall, a small wage and often generous tips, which made domestic servants better off than mature farm workers outside when all the benefits were added together and all this in a largely cashless society. But most important was the companionship within a disciplined society. By comparison village life was often brutal, lonely, rough and undernourished.

The people working in these often remote country houses — Longleat, Chatsworth, Kedleston and Seaton Delaval — were in self-contained worlds of their own far, even, from Warminster (and a life time away from Bath or Bristol) or Bakewell or Derby or Newcastle. It is not surprising that many of the women in domestic service remained unmarried; they did not wish to change the comforts and known routines of the great house for the homes of outdoor workers.

I think I know the reason why people talk in hushed, almost reverential whispers when they tour National Trust houses: there is no one real in them to talk to. I try to cast my mind back to the days when such houses were buzzing with life and activity until I am brought up startled with the thought: what did these houses smell like? I shall spare you the details of the lavatories, but think of all those unwashed bodies, even amongst the owners.

But the pace of the clock ticks on. Those Victorian villas on the south coast became guest houses and small hotels. Now they are being turned into "rest homes" for the elderly forgetting that the social, economic and domestic structure of a truly rural community is a paradox of both fragile and granite. And in this I detect an almost sinister new attitude; an increasing degree of alienation between "them and us" which is turning either into resentment or a detached "leave them to their own misfortune".

The imposition is by those who come and stay and make the country and coastal dwellers conform to that romanticised view of what suburbia believes the country should be, not what it is, often cold, gale-driven, wet, dirty, smelly, lonely, demanding of self-resources and, "would you believe it, darlings, the lawn is turning brown with the drought we get every summer. Now you think the council *would* do something about that, with *all* the rain we had last winter . . ."

A friend, an educated and articulate cowman — the farm craftsman or technician with at least £150,000 worth of equipment or animals invested in his skills and as his hourly responsibility, who regards the production line factory worker as today's clodhopping Hodge — commented that the takeover of parts of the countryside is a form of domestic colonisation.

"If the British returned to Black Africa and imposed the same morality and economics on the people there it would create uproar amongst liberal thinkers in parliament and orchestrated hatred at the United Nations," he said.

It is, of course, a gross and malicious exaggeration . . . but it has that un-nerving core of truth about it.

No, ours is not a beautiful village. It never was. In the 1850s it was hardly there at all. But by the 1950s it had been designated an "area of rural development". This turned out to be rather like an overweight lady without a girdle . . . the village sprawled. It found a role but lost its heart in doing so. Planners planned it but I suspect that planners could not plan a day of prayer in a monastery.

But a village is not what it looks like. Take a look at some of those picture postcard villages in Hampshire and Dorset with their medieval slums which appear on calendars throughout the world — and every time it rains water runs down the walls and new and ever more exotic varieties of fungus grow on the bedclothes every day. A village is the people who live in it, not its buildings.

It is this sense of time and timelessness which can pervade the countryside and remind us that we the inheritors are only tenants for life. We must improve what we have for the benefit of those who will come after us.

How did Repton and Kent and Lancelot Brown feel about building gardens they knew they would never see in the perfection of maturity? It was not simply a sense of time or a sense of destiny which made rich Georgian men want great houses in grand landscapes and a garden setting, the combination of the designs as a whole was little short of visionary. But there was also self-confidence where men could plant an oak tree in a park and know without question that future generations of their own families would enjoy their foresight. Does that self-confidence still exist in a society which appears to grasp at every straw of self-enrichment regardless of cost; that destroys the rain forests of Brazil to enlarge the deserts of the Sahara and makes tomorrow's Brazilian desert inevitable?

Time out of mind, time beyond imagination does exist ... if you go castle watching. No, the breeze has not blown my brains away and scattered them over the fields. Nor have the castles become as ephemeral as migrating birds, here in plenty now but mysteriously gone in a few moments.

The idea came to mind in Cornwall while I was a prisoner in a borrowed cottage, and as a gale screeched round the chimneys like a thousand hags on broomsticks and the rain, which seemed to start somewhere near Bermuda, crashed down from a mile high on to the thick slate roof.

The thought crossed my mind that on such a foul day there would be no tourists at Tintagel ... and there weren't. I thought that perhaps, alone, I might get a different feel for a ruined fortress possibly started in prehistoric times and which had outlived its military usefulness by the twelfth century. Would it be possible there, I wondered, to grasp the concept of "time out of mind". There is a beautifully romantic idea that if you listen carefully, properly tuned in, the stones of ancient buildings will speak to you, tell you their story, or even weep if murder has been carried out within their walls.

At Berkeley Castle where Edward II was brutally and perversely murdered — the legend is that they heard his screams in Berkeley village, which, although implausible, only adds to the whole macabre scene — the sense of chill and doom creeps into your body in that small room and the nearby corridors however sunny the day outside.

147

I have never had the same feeling in houses reputed to be wildly haunted.

At Tintagel, in a force ten gale, the stones whisper gently as you walk slowly through the bailey and across the bridge to the great hall on the island.

At Glastonbury they say that if you listen quietly you can hear King Arthur asleep under the Tor, waiting for the call if England needs him. He must sometimes recently have stirred in his sleep. It is a lot of rubbish really, isn't it? Except that so many people want such stories to be true.

My idea grew bigger when I stopped at Stonehenge. A party of school children were larking about, chirping like fledglings in bright sunlight and not the least bit interested in the great stones and their significance. I thought I would go back at dawn, it did not have to be a midsummer, druidical dawn.

It was cold; the sun rose wearily and the atmosphere of Stonehenge changed: morose, watching, even frightening. This was no longer a tourist wonder but a mathematical conundrum, a place of primitive worship and probably human sacrifice, a place of dread.

But why did I never feel the same sense of foreboding at Avebury Ring . . . could the Ring really be a sort of giant abacus to measure the passage of time, and through the angles of the sun longitude and latitude? Nor did I have this strange feeling at Avebury's sister ring at Castlerigg, on the bleak, snow-covered hills of Cumbria where, and I am not alone in suggesting this, some of the stones sprawled like portly drunkards in the snow.

But there were some castles which were ephemeral: after the great French invasion of 1545 castles were built at both East and West Cowes to make a strategic triangle and Portsmouth and Southampton Water and as a guard to the eastern approach of the Solent. The one on the east side has long since gone. The castle on the west side has been completely transformed from the stench of horses, the smell of soldiers in their crude leather tunics and the air blue with woodsmoke, to the refinements of one of the most exclusive clubs in the world, the Royal Yacht Squadron, but it is still known to Islanders (Vectensians) as "Cowes Castle".

The irony is that as a fortress it had one cannon; now there is a line of beautiful small cannons to start and end the racing as the yachts, as flibberty-gibberty as teenage girls at a party, twirl round the Solent under their vivid sails.

It is also said that King Henry's cannons gave the name to the twin town as they made noises like a cow lowing:

the two great cows, that in great thunder roar,
This on the eastern, that on the western shore . . .

Then on to one of the most spectacular of British castles at Carisbrooke where the donkey still walks the wheel with an almost historic solemnity to draw water from the well, and where a deep sense of tragedy oozes from every stone as you read of the fate of Charles I, a man who seemed only able to evoke deep love or violent hatred but nothing in between.

Looking down from the heights of the ramparts over the steep earth banks, too steep to climb, your heart should jump with joy at the sight of thousands of almost gaudy yellow cowslips smothering the banks.

Did the young Princess Elizabeth, a prisoner in the castle with her father, also peer over the ramparts at those cowslips; did they gladden her heart before she died so tragically young and was buried, humbly, in the town church?

The times changed and that element of mindless brutality passed. Men wanted windows in their castles as the threat of domestic war receded . . . just look at Leeds Castle in Kent and compare it with the brooding, sinister evil evoked by Hermitage Castle on the Scottish borders or the implied threat of Bamburgh.

The rest you know: the castles became the great houses of the landed magnates, the feudal lords had become "gentlemen".

But do not for one moment think that this experience of time encapsulated in stone is a British preserve: my daughter returned from an Adriatic cruise to Venice in, of all things no-one expects to find in Venice, a snowstorm. She was the only person on deck for what must have been a magical experience. "I expected Venice, with all its palaces and churches, to be beautiful," she said, and then she had to seek out the right words, "but in the snow the city had completely changed. You needed different words to describe it."

It was, I think, the stones that were speaking to her.

150

There is another dimension to a sense of time, of existing in both time and space, and it is in the experience of clear, uncluttered open space which appears not to have changed in centuries. Simple in concept, difficult in achievement.

It started like this: I was standing in a concrete and glass tomb on the edge of Green Park amongst the exhaust fumes of central London. Looking out of the window I saw a peregrine falcon hanging in the sky.

It really was a peregrine. Once you have seen a peregrine it is never forgotten. Its shape becomes etched on your eyes and in your memory.

On the edge of Windsor Forest a few days later a peregrine stooped out of the sky at speed — eighty miles an hour is nothing to this falcon — and hit a woodpigeon which seemed to explode in the air but which it failed to hold.

When I picked up the pigeon it was warm and dead, its back stripped as if plucked by a master gamekeeper. I would imagine that it was the easy pickings amongst feral pigeons and starlings which attracted the peregrine into central London. The argument that city skyscrapers are the cliffs and canyons of their natural habitat has always been a prediction as most carnivorous birds are opportunistic rather than calculating on the combination of territory, food, mating and nestings sites, although I do not for one moment decry the attempts to get them to nest on the BBC television building at Wood Lane. It was suggested, incidentally, that the Windsor Forest peregrine nested in the private and largely unvisited part of the Forest, but no substantial evidence was ever produced to support this idea.

What is beyond question is that nature creates efficient machines for killing — the variable geometry of the peregrine's wings; the stealth of a stoat or the swaggering bustle of the badger with paws more efficient than a mechanical digger.

As I held the pigeon I started to wonder about other falcons and hawks on mountain and sea-coast cliffs. I had seen black kites in Germany. Children used to hand feed the kites on old London Bridge before the Great Fire of London in 1666 when they were common scavengers in the sewage and garbage cluttered streets of the City and, incidentally, it was most likely to have been smoke pollution rather than persecution which drove these birds out of London. I had also seen many fish-eating buzzards in Switzerland, and kestrels and sparrowhawks have been commonplace in my life although probably the biggest day was the discovery of Hobbies in Berkshire . . . but what about red kites?

Off we went to Aberystwyth, that Victorian architectural jewel with its sad remnants of a castle and the happy remains of a cliff-side graveyard, the ancient car loaded with wife, children, dog, cat and rabbits to stay in one of those caravans which are as luxurious as a millionaire's yacht.

In the sullen hills the rain hits you viciously, each drop stabbing at your face and you find yourself, suddenly, knee-deep in a bog. Then, overhead, between the mewing of a buzzard, distant as a piece of cloud

152

above the rain, there was the sound of grunting that suggests a herd of pigs is flying overhead: ravens.

The ravens were talking to each other on the wing as excitedly as two old dears on a shopping expedition, and they were heading up a rocky escarpment towards a flat-topped mountain.

I settled into the wet tussocks to watch. My wife had taken refuge in the car with a book; the smallest child had set off along a road which led to nowhere and eventually returned and announced that fact, and my son, I discovered later and too late, had fed my lunch-time sandwiches to a pair of Mallard on the tarn.

Then I saw something which has puzzled me ever since, puzzled me not because it is an uncommon observation but because no one has yet provided an adequate answer, one raven peeled away and flew below the mountain top, the other flew up the escarpment until it was hit by the wind slicing over the flat top.

Caught by that savage wind, the raven tumbled backwards, head over heels for a hundred feet while his friend, was it his girl friend, flew underneath still grunting like a sow at lunchtime. Then it was her turn. Up she flew to be knocked sideways by the wind, rolling her over and over, while he soared against the skerries, grunting continuously as if he were laughing his black, bewhiskered head off.

But this was not a game of the moment. It went on for over two hours to the obvious enjoyment, even merriment, of those lovable and flopping birds.

It raises the question which the watchers of the sky have never been able to answer: do animals play? And if they do play, do they derive the same creative and imaginative development that children get, for whom play is an essential part of development, whether they are playing alone or in company?

I stayed and watched the ravens buffet themselves in the cold autumn gale until I was driven home by cold and wet. The ritual of fun was taking place as it must have done, unseen by prying humans, for centuries; and even now I can hear the croaking laughter of those huge birds.

A peregrine on those cliffs watched these buffoons with a cold eye — how it is possible for a bird to stand motionless for so long while the hours slip by into that eternity of time and spacc?

Magpies flew by . . .

> One for sadness
> two for joy
> three for a girl
> four for a boy
> five for silver
> six for gold
> seven for a secret
> which can't be told.

In deference to time honoured tradition (and to keep your luck in your pocket) you raise your hat three times on seeing the first magpie of the day and say three times, "Good morning, my lord". Is this an invocation of the Holy Trinity again, and if so, why? The peregrine did not even turn its head and the ravens carried on their loopy game as if their cousins did not exist.

But what about the red kites? I never saw one on that expedition. I went back for three consecutive years, fully briefed by bird-watchers of international renown and never saw a red kite. It was not that the red kites were not there, it is simply — and you get no prizes for guessing this — that I am too easily distracted. Then, one day, in a flat valley miles from anywhere pretentious enough to call itself a mountain we saw them over gentle fields with grazing cattle.

It was a thrilling sight, but for reasons I cannot readily explain it was not the same as watching those ravens putting on a cabaret in the driving rain.

CHAPTER
TEN

How Dark the Forest

She bore herself with all the dignity of those who are close to death, know it and are unafraid.

Sometime earlier that year she had been chasing a hare without a chance of catching it over deep plough, that is the sort of thing which goes on in greyhounds' minds, and had hit a strand of barbed wire, the curse of the English countryside. She spun through the air, all arms and legs, like an animated wheel and, on reaching home, had the three-cornered tear in her skin, like a gash in a pair of old trousers, stitched up. (If you own animals you soon learn, out of necessity, the rudiments of veterinary science.) The hare escaped, as if that were of any consequence, and we thought nothing more of the incident. The greyhound quickly recovered, a small brindled bitch with a rather winning narrow face. In the fullness of time she was taken to the dog-hound and took, and nature seemed to be following its natural, happy course.

Then we noticed a lump on her shoulder. It grew rapidly and the quandary, a crisis for our consciences, was whether to operate on the cancer and risk the lives of the pups — bitches at the right stage of gestation can give birth through Caesarean section — or to let nature take its inevitable and saddening course, a real race of time against creeping disease.

Towards the end, heavy in pup, the cancer on her shoulder as big as a football and so unsightly we kept her away from other humans, she could just get about but only with the greatest difficulty but, thank goodness, apparently without pain. Then, in the night, she whelped, the usual messy struggle and she mothered the pups, drawing them in to her for their first and greedy feed. Two days later, still striving to bring her pups from darkness into the sighted world, she silently died.

It is utterly wrong to attribute human feelings, emotions and responses to animals if only for the fact that it masks our understanding of animals, but I am convinced that the brindle bitch willed herself to live long after the disease would normally have crushed her spirit and sapped her body. The inner life force compelled her to produce that one litter in her short life, her own footnote to posterity. Perhaps it is equally wrong to speculate that she may have died, equally uncomplainingly, but prematurely if she had not been carrying that package of undistinguished whippersnappers. The instinct to survive, I sometimes think, is stronger in animals than in many humans. Indeed, the instincts of the dark forests of pre-history keep coming through animals into the bright world of our electronic civilisation.

These thoughts came to mind when Anya appeared out of nowhere to take up residence in the spare room ... and every other room with her bouncing, popping, laughing young self. She had arrived complete with battered suitcase and a brace of little Lord Fauntleroys named Charlie and Feliks, direct descendants, from the damage they caused in the house, from Attila the Hun and his many friends and relations.

The cats were born in a block of high-rise flats somewhere in the urban tundra of London. They had never seen a field, nor even a garden border and yet, when the sand tray was set out they homed in on it as if the instructions for use were clearly written on the side of the old seed tray. Then they would very carefully run their fore-paws over the protective newspapers laid out on the floor as if covering their droppings with earth. No one told them how to do it or why it should be done. The instinct was born into them even if they got it wrong at first. But the genes of generations did not let them down.

Then we were all thrown into a state of utter panic. The cow had calved. We knew that by the bellowing in the night. But could we find the calf? Children and dogs quartered the barnground field, then Brumbles and Stairs and the wrongly-named Ten Acres, until, tucked away in a corner in a loose patch of tall grass we found her alive and healthy.

While we searched, it was hardly even dawn and a mad artist had slashed at the sky with vermilion paint to light our search, the cow, named Margaret, kept coming between us, menacingly, working hard to keep us away, protecting the sleeping, new-dropped calf. Wherever we moved she moved. She was a mirror image of our actions and she spoke to us with a voice as brash as a bass trombone.

Instinct prevailed in her over domesticity. She was, for that time, a wild animal even though we all know that the cow has been farmed and domesticated for thousands of years.

Stumbling over fallow deer fawns lying-up in shrubby land in the New Forest with the doe circling cruelly close and likely to attack at any moment — you must always take care of dogs in deer country especially when the rut is on and before the calves are fully mobile — there can be an understanding of the primitive territorial and protective nature of truly wild animals. With deer you have only to see the rutting pit and the savage slashing of trees that mark territories to understand how close to the surface this instinctive behaviour lives. But when it appears in farm animals it is a different sort of revelation.

Then the mare produced a colt foal and there was great rejoicing in the house at the prospect of another willing hand to help with the work. In a gentle way I would play a game of pretending to touch the foal but without diminishing my authority over either animal.

The mare would do her best not to let me handle the foal. With majestic, almost balletic speed she would come between us and the foal and she would look at me with that expression which says: "I shall kick you if you touch my foal".

Man wins. After a few days of isolation in a sheltered valley, more a cleft in the hills, the colt had to be stabled and the mare followed behind, head down, knowing that the game was over. She is a thinking animal. But I was careful not to belittle the mare. It was her foal, not mine.

Then there is the kennel of Welsh springer spaniels. Jenny had become so aged and infirm that in charity she had to be put down. Her daughter, Susan, (whoever calls a spaniel Susan?) died within ten days. She died for no reason known to man. She simply pined away despite all the love and affection we could give her and all the attention paid to her. The bond between animal and animal had been broken and we are fools if we do not understand how deep that bond runs or how long an animal's memory can be. There is, for instance, the well authenticated case of the two brewery horses which were conscripted to the front in France in World War I and returned to England, fortunately uninjured, four years later. On being unharnessed each horse walked calmly, not simply to the same stable it had left, but to the same stall in that stable. Conditioning you may call it; memory you may call it, but whatever it is, it is truly astonishing.

The death of an animal hurts us: we live close to our animals. When a dog had to be destroyed — death, so to speak, is a fact of life in the country — all the children came to the vet's to place their hands on him as the needle went in. The eldest said that as she had lived with him throughout her life she would be with him at the end. There was no unhappiness, they had enjoyed their long friendship and the bond between human and animal had been struck with a ring of steel for life. Do you wonder that that girl rides like a dream, jumps any fence and approaches any horse, however ill-tempered and

bad-mannered, as if she is approaching an elderly aunt
. . . with courtesy and respect, but never with diffidence.

All this leads me to believe that we underestimate
both the intelligence and instinctive response in animals
that can be turned to human advantage.

When we kept a herd of eighty Guernsey milkers they
did not have to be called, they waited at the appointed
hour in the collecting yard and in strict order of
precedence; as there are "pack leaders" amongst fox
hounds there are herd leaders amongst cattle. Margaret
would come first with all the bustle and self-importance
of an over-burdened lady trying to get on a narrow
country bus, Peggy second . . . and Peggy would go into
stall five. There was nothing on earth you could do —
shouting, raving, pushing, shoving, even doing handstands
round the yard — that would make her take another stall
in the milking parlour, and so the ritual went on twice in
every day with Thin Lizzie, a sort of bovine Worzel
Gummage of a cow, inevitably last, like a naughty
schoolgirl, and always facing the wrong direction, both
last and least in the herd.

And I believe these cows could count: try giving two
pitchers of cow cake to a three-pitcher cow and you get
a mouthful of abuse that would impress the proverbial
fishwife. They watch you with such care; perhaps we
fail with animals by not looking more closely into their
eyes . . . Mirrors of the soul someone said.

But you may be as intellectual as you like about
animals, and study all the vast zoological books on
animal behaviour but they mean not a thing to our
Virginia — about as inapt a name for a female cat as

anyone can invent. Her legendary promiscuity would bring the guiles of harlotry into disrepute, and to prove her point she had four black and matching kittens in the dark, comfortable and heated airing cupboard. However did she get into the house? Her home is the farmyard — definitely. It was a fairly messy job, but after a moment's thought we felt it in our hearts that we should forgive her. She was only responding to instinct.

Stories of what appears to be constructive intelligence in animals abound. This assumes that such intelligence is limited to quadrupeds. This is not so. For most of my life I have been fascinated by the crow family, not because they are common but probably because they are so obvious. They are a monstrous legion.

A pair of crows took possession of the oak tree at the bottom of the garden like squatters in an empty house. I hoped this noisy pair would not stay although they were with us all the winter, swooping down close to the house to snatch pieces of fat thrown out for the younger, smaller birds.

Then, although they fly off to forage in barren and distant fields, they started setting out their nesting territory which appears to be little more than half an acre. They fly to the highest points they can find and bellow at each other, move on to the next point and start all over again. This duet which sounds like iron grating on iron goes on most of the morning in a single key.

I have always been leery of the crow family with the exception of the jackdaw which adopted us. He lived wild, but in the mornings I would call him and he would usually land, painfully, on my bald head, his claws well dug in. He would come inside and have his food, then he would ride on the carriage of my typewriter as I worked in the window, shouting and squawking as the keys thundered upwards. But sometimes he would travel "with his back to the engine" and I would have to clean the manuscript paper — frequently. Then he would preen before flying to the top of the bookcase where he would sleep. Sometimes he would settle in the crook of my arm, as I sat in an armchair, and sleep even as I moved my arms to turn the pages of the *Daily Telegraph*. Well, at least he was not stealing paper clips and hiding them down the sides of chairs, or tearing pieces of cooking foil to shreds in the kitchen to hide in vases of dried flowers. But whatever their many charms, at the end of the day you have to admit that having a jackdaw indoors is a very messy pastime and not in the least likely to endear you to the ladies of the house. The Jackdaw of Rheims had greater respect . . .

> He sat on the Cardinal's chair
> Bishop and abbot and prior were there . . .
> With a great many more of lesser degree
> In sooth a goodly company . . .

While this family may well be good company we are most certainly of "lesser degree" and were invited to a neighbour's for that most civilised pastime, sipping chilled wine in a summer garden. I tied a piece of string round one of the jackdaw's legs with careful knots. He watched this with his head on one side and a beady eye glinting and before we had got ten yards down the road

he had untied all the knots and flown away into a tree
. . . his favourite tree from which he would swoop down
and land on the heads of ladies as they passed
unsuspectingly by; shouts and squeals, dropped shopping and me hiding in the garden scared to appear and
own up in case I got a bash round the head from a
handbag. Jackdaws are quite acceptable here, it is the
ladies who are untamed . . .

Later, the jackdaw, like his cousin from France, joined
the open-air feasting, his eyes fixed on any piece of
costume jewellery glittering in the summer sun.

Very partial to liver pâté was my jackdaw and also to
bathing in the dog's drinking bowl every other day, but
with such delight and splashing that the floor was soon
awash. Once finished in the tub he would fly onto the
kitchen table and shake himself like a retriever, making
a new flood.

For all their obvious talents, I do not ascribe quite the
jackdaw's intelligence to rooks. A friend had one with a
mathematical turn of mind: he had one of those Russian
dolls which unscrewed to reveal other dolls inside that.
First he would put them in a line and the rook would
place each one into the next in the correct order; then
the dolls would be mixed up and the rook would, and
just as quickly, put them all together in the right order.
But his true party trick was to find a button carefully
hidden under one of the upturned halves and then
jumbled up with the others. Inevitably he went straight
to the correct half. What puzzled him was to craftily
remove one of the pieces. He would assemble the halves
until he found one was missing and simply stop.

Another aspect which belied their apparent lack of intelligence was demonstrated at the local rookery which was about a mile away and always the source of much arguing and shouting before nesting started. Perhaps they were jockeying for position, to be "king of the castle"; perhaps there were struggles to reclaim the family home although I have never found any evidence that rooks return to exactly the same nest as in previous years or generations. The puzzle was that the rookery was in what used to be a magnificent stand of elm trees until *Scolytus scolytus*, the beetle which carried the devastating Dutch elm disease, arrived. Why rooks have always preferred elm trees is another of life's mysteries which has not been revealed to us yet.

There is a common old wives' tale that the rooks can predict when a tree is going to fall, and they leave for a new site. Let me dispel that story and tell you here and now that the rooks were not listening when the old wives gossiped. These rooks were still planning to nest in trees long dead with the disease. Come a great gale sweeping up the Channel non-stop from five hundred miles west of the Scillies, what the elders in the pub tend to call a "hooligan" rather than a hurricane, and the rooks were clinging to the branches like seamen on the yards of a windjammer rounding the Horn. And down came two trees, rooks and all. Tenaciously they started all over again, but this time in living trees.

It would have been sad if they had deserted the village; a village without a rookery is hardly a village at all, but in many parts of the country their numbers are declining though as much the result of change in agricultural methods on arable land as a lack of suitable trees.

But there are two members of this crow family I do not like to see around the house, much as I get a real physical kick out of seeing choughs on the sea cliffs on that little piece of the Welsh coast where they still nest, and the thought of seeing flocks of choughs on the sea cliffs of southern Portugal is almost enough to make me sell-up house and home and head south. My unconcealed dislike is reserved for jays and magpies. Beautiful he may be, but the jay can be tempted to eat both the eggs and the fledglings of songbirds. I watched one move down the hazel hedge. There was no question that he was quietly, secretly and stealthily looking for nests. The blackbird was nesting in a clipped bay tree. You can, and I do, hold a small child just a few inches from her and she will not desert the nest but the harrowing of the Jay drives her off.

Most of all I dislike Magpies. They are voracious thieves of other bird's eggs and I am surprised that there has been so little comment on the ease with which they have adapted to suburban life. I was told that in suburbia they have learned to open egg boxes left on the doorstep with the morning's milk.

Dr Brewer of "Phrase and Fable" fame says that in the Westcountry people used to spit three times — could this be another protective reference to the Holy Trinity — when one was sighted, and in Scotland when one was sighted flying near the windows it foretold death. In Sweden and a number of other places, they were connected with witchcraft as familiars.

Quite why this dramatic bird has been adopted so widely into country lore throughout Europe is a mystery, but the evidence of so many dialect stories suggests that the magpie, often as an omen of evil, did not come from a single source. The variations of the nursery rhyme tell this tale:

> One is sorrow, two is mirth,
> Three is a wedding, four is a birth,
> Five is a christening, six is a death,
> Seven is heaven, eight is hell
> And nine for the devil and his ane sel . . .

Another variation, more common in southern Britain, says:

> One for sadness, two for joy,
> Three for a girl, four for a boy
> Five for silver, six for gold,
> Seven for a secret that can't be told . . .

But ends differently:

> . . . Eight for a kiss, nine for wish;
> Ten for a meeting not to be missed . . .

Then there are moments of pure magic and merriment amongst birds. We were trudging down a muddy lane on a bitterly cold day when one of the children — the one with a nose for trouble — poked her head through a farm gate. There, in broad daylight, in stubbles on an unploughed headland, marching and counter-marching like a small army of miniature soldiers were about twenty short-eared owls, grazing. They walk absolutely upright, as if they have been told, as I was in the army, to march with the shoulders back and "bags of swank".

But wherever you go there is simply no escaping that pestilential visitation called crows: Charles and Lynda bought a house of deceptive but unspecified antiquity in a quiet corner of Bishopsdale in north Yorkshire where their dale starts to flirt with Wensleydale, and only a short walk over the featureless hills from the shattering silence of Coverdale.

The antiquity of Mill Scar and its barns and byres, the tiny single stable for a small Fell pony and the stone-built pig sty where the solitary hen laid its breakfast egg, had even crept and lain dormant for many decades in the kitchen where there was a cooking range which was probably pre-Victorian but, unlike most, utterly inefficient. A new range had to be bought but the chimneys, lined with random rubble, had to be sleeved otherwise Lynda's guests would have enjoyed everlasting sleep as the fumes from the new fire seeped into the rooms.

The chimney was blocked. Within minutes every room was filled with poisonous smoke and we fled into the garden. Up went the builder and down came a century's worth of debris, including seventeen dead jackdaws, all in feather and all as solid as the stone which had entombed them, mummified by the gentle smoke of the old range.

How long had they been there? And were there really only seventeen? It was easy enough to know how they got there. At any time from spring to late summer there might be a jackdaw perched on the edge of a chimney pot peering down the abyss with nesting in mind. There is not a crevice in the sand seacliffs here which does not have a grey-naped head peering out like a lady on a Victorian Lancashire doorstep gossiping with her neighbours, except that invariably jackdaws shout at their friends and neighbours.

What I cannot understand is how a bird can be so suicidally stupid as to explore a bottomless chimney while its relatives perform miracles of memory. The man who kept the pub up by my local railway station when I lived in surburban London, had a commuting jackdaw which went noisily — until you have owned a jackdaw you have no idea how noisy and demanding they are — up to Waterloo on the 8.12 deep in conversation with human commuters, and came home later in the day when it happened to suit him.

Now, how can a jackdaw work out which train goes from Waterloo station with some twenty platforms, hundreds of trains a day, a jungle of noise, machinery and hustling people, down to a suburban backwater such as Teddington. It is not that every train runs from the same platform; they run in an irregular pattern from platforms one to five, some travelling the loop line through Richmond and back to the high number platforms of Waterloo while others go, less frequently, through Teddington to Shepperton. But he always got home, much to our annoyance, even though it was reported that he would sometimes end up at Chessington and have to fly home over the park. But, in that case,

169

how did he know that Chessington was the terminus of that particular suburban line and how, in the first instance, did he know he was at Teddington and not alight at Hampton Wick or Strawberry Hill? The mystery deepens until it is revealed that even this jackdaw, with all his displays of intelligence, had a fatal flaw.

One day he simply got it all wrong. Having harangued the tired commuters and spotted a few striped suits — jackdaws are incredibly messy birds — he dashed out of the window as the train pulled into Teddington station ... straight into the 5.40 to Shepperton as it went zipping by.

We were not exactly heart-broken. He would perch, conversationally, on the edge of half filled glasses and capsize them, which was very good for the publican's business but did little to endear him to the customers. Endearment is not the name of the game. At Holy Trinity, Bembridge, chicken wire was put over the gilded arms and Roman numerals of the clock because the jackdaws, with an armful of twigs, nested in the clock which promptly stopped. Evicting these squatters is a costly job with ladders to hire and men to employ.

But chicken wire or no chicken wire, the jackdaws nested in the clock the following year and the long-serving vicar's warden was seen dancing about in the churchyard, pointing speechlessly at the violator of ecclesiastic timepieces.

The vicar of Blackstock, in the diocese of Chelmsford, a charitable man of forgiving nature, decided to inspect the fabric of his church on his appointment to the living. He climbed the steep ladder up to the Silence Chamber immediately below the belfry. This is that wonder of instinctive science which allowed the unskilled and unlettered to hang the bells to be heard far away over the parish, but muffles the sound so that the bells can be scarcely heard inside the church itself, and all the more intriguing at Blackstock as its tower is wooden, the largest in Britain.

But the trapdoor would not at first open. Over generations, who could count how many, the jackdaws had come and, having increased their numbers, as the good book admonishes us all to do, they went, leaving behind an ever deepening mattress of elm twigs ... the builder's men took forty barrow loads away before the room was empty and the arras windows could be wired up, and I wondered why the mystical figure of forty should feature yet again in a church.

But to return to Charles and Lynda: Jackdaws have no difficulty getting into a chimney. To them it is just another nesting place, but bright as they are they cannot get out. Attracted by the light above, they try to struggle upwards, but their wings are wrongly constructed to climb up a narrow chamber in which they cannot extend their wings. Like most birds they die of stress before they are physically exhausted or injured.

The release from this trap is simple and applies to any other bird, especially those daft Tawny owls which fell headlong down the broad chimneys of our Georgian farmhouse when I was a child. The answer is to take a sheet of white paper, newspaper will do, fix it over the narrowing aperture of the fireplace and put a strong electric torch under it to shine upwards and attract the Jackdaw or Speleologist owl downwards. Be careful or the suicidal bird will be flying round your room showering everything with soot, dust and droppings; crashing into pictures, knocking ornaments off the tables and hurtling flowers to the floor. Well, it is better than finding seventeen mummies stuffed up the kitchen flue, isn't it?

Having concluded that perhaps jackdaws are not as clever as I had imagined, I then saw something which has long since defied explanation. Taking a detour through Windsor Great Park I stopped amongst those bluff, tangle-armed oaks which have seen a millennium of monarchs travel from gaudy and gold into dust. It was late spring, some might say a typical English spring; there was a fierce and cold wind and a crowd of about thirty Jackdaws in one oak, some apparently unconcerned in the high branches, some on the rough cut grass while a small group of about ten lined a low branch.

One by one, to the encouragement of their friends they, like the ravens in the Welsh mountains, tumbled cartwheeling headlong into the wind to be buffeted and thrown until they landed in the grass where they looked upwards for the approval of their friends. And this game went on endlessly. Sometimes one would get tired of the game and would fly listlessly off to a neighbouring tree or sit quietly and preen. But another would take its place and those that seemed reluctant to play were loudly encouraged to take the plunge into the wind. They poised on the edge of the branch, tottering on the hands of the wind, and the shouts and cawing increased until the reluctant bird launched itself. Above, the gallery to which you might imagine the buffoons and tumblers might be playing, ignored their antics as if they and the elaborate game did not exist. Only the few birds on the playing branch were as interested as I ... but I have always been intrigued by the dark mysteries of the forests.

CHAPTER
ELEVEN

Travelling Gentlemen

There is only one way to find out. Do it yourself. If you do not ask the right questions how can you expect to discover the right answers?

I was never sure about hunting; the organised chase of animals with hounds, the breeding of birds — grouse, pheasant, partridge — the coursing of hares, even sea fishing . . . I was never sure.

But I had to find out for myself.

So I went hunting and with the exception of deer stalking and otter hunting I have seen it all now. Ferreting, lamping, long netting, ratting, I just had to know for myself; I would never rely on other people's words or their experiences so, starting as a boy, an escapee from school, I went to look for myself. I may have some doubts, some reservations, but I, at very least, took part. I saw for myself.

We unboxed hounds at Chale Green. Chale Green was a happening, not a place. There was once a pub on the green. Now it has gone, and I feel very sorry for the people who live on the green. A locality without a pub is like a village without a rookery, it has no heart.

Taking hounds to old plough on rising ground we soon found a hare which went off at 1,000 volts over the brow and was not to be seen for half an hour. But we were soon in the business of finding her with Denys Danby, one of the finest teachers of the mysteries and good manners of beagling to us boys, thundering ahead.

Mr Danby hunted hounds to watch them hunt. I believe to this day that he was embarrassed when they killed a hare, even on that famous moon-lit December night at Bathingbourne when she was "dragged down" (why are all hares "females"?) at seven at night, having been hunted for an entire afternoon.

"Watch them cast," Danby would whisper. "Watch them cast left-hand. Cast my beauties, cast slow." And this man of huge physical stature would almost tremble with pleasure, his arms hovering at his side like an albatross on the wing.

Or he would stand over a hare in the form, gazing down at her with infinite wonder then retreating a full hundred yards before putting hounds on. "Cast forward my little beauties," he would say in the sort of endearing voice most men would reserve for their mistresses.

But on this day our hare went down into The Wilderness; a bewildering flat valley of osiers, white willows, silver birch and black alders. It floods up to a foot in depth in winter and the whole vast acreage becomes a snakes and ladders of narrow paths through undergrowth where cattle went down to the summer stream to drink, and stood on those balmy days of our bird-watching while they watched us with that timeless melancholy which cows alone seem to possess. But The

Wilderness when flooded was a nightmare without signposts, a dream of endless terror.

We lost half the field. Most, dry footed, took to the refuge of the hilltops where they could look down on the sudden eruptions of hounds and followers and their equally sudden disappearance into the swamps and the trees.

You beagle, I quickly learned, in sandshoes, not dinky little red wellies or posh brogues which retain the water. On Brading Marshes the previous week, Denys Danby crossed the River Yar breaking the ice in front of him with his blackthorn thumb-stick to head off hounds running into a field of in-lamb ewes. As the water closed around his chest my wife turned and headed for home. It was rumoured that she was heard to be muttering, no doubt about getting the dinner into the oven.

But here, in The Wilderness, the hare showed quite extraordinary intelligence. Round and round those narrow flooded channels she flew at a hand canter. As she came down a waterlogged path we pushed back into the undergrowth to let her pass as pedestrians would on a country lane when a juggernaut thunders through. But not once or twice; ears laid back, not even bothering to look up at us — we humans were no danger — but followed by hounds in ever diminishing numbers, she plunged through this maze, often appearing to scamper across the very surface of the water while the hounds, and certainly the human element, stumbled through the water.

My pal, Charlie Wallace, the man who invented tangental thinking, that is the ability to think sideways but never backwards or forwards, even stood over the path with legs apart so that both hare and hounds galloped underneath the arch. Then he turned around the other way, again making an arch for the hare and eventually the hounds to come back the other way.

The hare was finally seen, as wet and exhausted and as attractive as a 'flu victim's handkerchief, loping over the next brow, the one we had not thought about. It took half an hour for the whips to gather in the hounds — whip them in would have been a bad misnomer for a pack which was now spread over fifty acres of flooded land — and get them on the line again. Off we went, our clothes drying out in the freezing wind, fears of being permanently disfigured by frost-bite receding as warmth came back to running feet.

Within sight of Whitecroft Psychiatric Hospital the hounds were called off; she was lost, or perhaps she had taken refuge inside; "A haven is a haven even from the real world", Charlie said. We hunted back to Chale Green in a desultory and totally unrewarded manner; there did not appear to be a single hare left on the Isle of Wight, and long before we reached the Green, we were engulfed in darkness and the entire field, one master, one huntsman, two whips and two young men, held hounds close up on narrow and dangerous lanes against unsuspecting cars already off for an evening with "Nutty" Edwards at Shorwell, or at the Three Bishops and the Blacksmith's Arms where murder had once taken place. Then there was the breaking of a bale of straw in which the hounds would luxuriate on the homeward journey.

"What time is it, Charlie?" the Master asked. There was a long silence. "Do you mean now?" Charlie replied, his capacity for tangental thinking never deserting him even after a hard day in the hunting field. His question was followed by an even longer silence before he continued: "I don't know. I haven't got a watch". Then he said, looking up into the endless cold of the black sky; "Pity we didn't kill today; we hunted hard".

The Master was lifting hounds into the box. Charlie was watching him. If you have mastered tangental thinking it would never occur to you to actually help, not even help a Master of Foot Hounds. "It isn't important to kill," the Master said in his usual quiet voice. "It is important to ask ourselves if we have enjoyed the day. Well, have you?"

Cold, wet, covered in mud and tired beyond words of expression, we thanked Mr Danby and the ever-present kennel huntsman, Teddy, for providing such a fascinating day.

Sixteen miles as we ran, the Master estimated. Who would ever guess how many miles the hounds and the hare ran? Who would ask *them* if they had enjoyed their day? Certainly we had to whip them on, and long after December darkness had engulfed the Island in its grip of iron, we had to whip them off.

I got home nearer nine than eight. My wife had spent the afternoon in warmth and comfort. "We ran all the way from Chale Green, through The Wilderness to the very walls of Whitecroft Psychiatric Hospital," I said

178

triumphantly, reaching for the decanter. "How appropriate," she said, smiling sweetly and picking up her knitting.

I knew that eventually I would have to own up. Come clean, so to speak, and tell the truth about how close we had sailed to the rocks of disaster, lured not by a gorgeous siren or a mermaid with a comb and a looking glass in her hand . . . it can happen, you know, as it happened to Matthew Trewhella who was lured into the sea at Pendour Cove, 350 feet below the fifteenth-century church at Zennor, where the event, mermaid and all, is commemorated in a carving on one of the pew ends. It is said that she admired his singing in the church, but what, I wonder did he see in her?

Well, the truth was this: we were facing financial ruin. While you were all throwing your money at the bulls and stags of the stock market to say nothing of the bears, and buying yachts with the profits, we bought two in-pup greyhounds. It was not, financially, a good idea although there were other, incalculable, compensations.

The first purchase was a sister of a greyhound Oaks winner. She immediately produced seven pups which returned the vast sum we paid for her. We knelt in the straw — why do bitches always whelp at two o'clock in the morning (like mares) and in temperatures which only eskimos can tolerate — and handled these hot tots of dogs and our praise to the bitch was unstinting.

As she mothered them she was told that to both the family and the national economy, to say nothing of the entire sporting world, she was an asset. She was, my brother declared proudly, "worth a guinea a box".

Characteristically, she drew back her lips showing a mouthful of fine white teeth and smiled at us. We could have kissed her.

The second hound, also in pup to a famous sire, was sold to us on the spurious grounds that she would make our fortune. Her progeny eventually won a race worth £4, but in doing so we met a large number of talkative travelling gentlemen with strong sporting interests but who did not appear to own a razor blade between them, and whose blue serge suits looked, shall we say, world weary. The night out cost £20. Hardly a profit by anyone's standards.

The point was that against all canine odds she managed to produce just one single brindle pup. Although not unknown, in young and normally fertile bitches this is quite unusual. You are a complete and hopeless failure we said; a stupid bitch we added in our disappointment.

She lay in the straw and drew back her lips and smiled at us and we all would have kissed her. She is beautiful and money is not important when you have a greyhound bitch which smiles at you.

Then I made the mistake, a terrible mistake, of transferring the language of the kennels and the countryside to a suburban drawing room. Without thinking I described a lady as a "hard bitch". Down here that is a considerable compliment. We have dogs and bitches and no one would wrongly describe the two. We have horses, mares, geldings, donkeys, mules and hinnies. Country people are, if nothing else, precise in their definitions of animals all the way from never making the mistake of asking a master of foxhounds how many dogs he has — they are hounds and are counted in couples, an odd one being a half couple — to a "sounder" of pigs or a skulk of foxes. And, in case you are asking, a hinny is the reverse of a mule being the product of a stallion and a she-ass.

But there was an interesting side product to this rash investment in racing greyhounds because we went off to the races at a country stadium. To say that this stadium was run down was the equal to throwing a casual insult at a scrap metal yard in saying that it was untidy.

Each of the children was given 20p to bet on each of the six races. Teach them the evils of gambling and drink early in life we said. My goodness, they were good pupils.

The smallest child promptly invested her place money on a huge and foul smelling hamburger complete with onions, brown sauce, tomato sauce, salt, pepper, mustard and vinegar. This was supplemented by a bag of chips. The middle child studied the card and looked closely at each hound as if he were the chief scrutineer and lost his money on every race including the one in which our greyhound was running . . . it was not his turn to win £4. The eldest child, armed with a pocket calculator and notebook, elbowed her way through the knot of unshaven travelling gentlemen in blue suits, and announced in language more suitable in the petty officer's mess than the drawing room that the bookies were not offering attractive enough odds for a young lady to invest her 20p.

She then promptly worked out the return after tax on a cross double at eleven to four on. It was a calculation which would have taken me a month to conclude and even then I would not have been sure of the accuracy of the answer. She got the odds right but her predictions were all unplaced. At least she had lost her money semi-scientifically and from that day to this none of the children has ever placed another bet. Now they pocket the money and quickly disappear into the crowd.

So we decided to run our own private race track in the high field, known unwisely as "Ten Acres", running the hare, an old sock filled with rabbit skins, from a car engine and with hand-opened traps. We invited our friends and their greyhounds, a collection which would have brought tears to the eyes of a professional trainer.

We had a maximum run of only 300 yards, we are still finding measuring distances in metres a little puzzling down here, and the eldest and most scientific child infuriated us all by consistently talking in metric measure and then asking if we wanted that "translated into English". This run did not give us much scope and as we had whippets, greyhounds, Afghan hounds — known to the children as "cheesehounds" from the day one jumped on to the kitchen table and scoffed the week's supply of cheese — a Tibetan spaniel with the most amazing Chippendale front end we had ever seen and a speed too slow to be measured in miles, or even kilometres, per hour, and a basset hound, it was only marginally less well organised than the local race track.

Large sums of money — at least by our standards but certainly not by the standards of the talkative travelling gentlemen who had pockets full of grubby banknotes which flashed from hand to hand in the mêlée around the bookmakers' stands — changed hands at our exclusive private race track until someone looked vaguely up at the clouds in the summer sky and announced in a confident voice that the village pub was open. Racing was promptly cancelled for the rest of the day.

CHAPTER
TWELVE

The Last Temptation

There was never a game that was worth a rap
For a rational man to play
Into which no accident or mishap could possibly
Find its way . . .

Adam Lindsay Gordon

It was a chance encounter in the dark. Driving down the Roman road that rose and fell over the high ground with the pleasing rhythm of a moving caterpillar, the barn owl, like a feather-filled pillowcase, was caught in the headlights so close to the car that I could see the brown speckling in his plumage as the impact of the air pushed forward by the car tossed him over the loaded roof rack.

Another needless death on the road?

I brought the car to a dangerous halt, swung over the grass curb, waking the passengers in the middle seat and returned to the scene of the accident. There in the faded moonlight stood the owl on a short fence post. He was shaking his head and peering round nervously, as if he had been walloped by a frying pan. I concluded that he was unhurt and probably only shocked and that peace, quiet and a lesson in curb drill were all that he needed.

Another night, turning a bend to the shute leading to the winding road which skirts the marshes, a badger, fortunately at a safe distance, scampered across the road — the speed at which badgers run never ceases to amaze me — like a stunted old man in baggy trousers. He looked neither left nor right and was gone so quickly my passenger did not even take in what he had seen.

To most people a badger is a badger is a badger just like any other badger. To those of us to whom a badger is a weekly, if not a daily encounter, every badger is different in colour, size, gait and personality. Keeping your eye on the countryside is not the ability to recognise species from a book but their whereabouts by noise or smell, the marking of territories by the droppings; scent for example is the dominant factor in rabbits' territorial identifications. It is also the immediate recognition of a bird from a fraction of a second's glimpse, perhaps in silhouette against a darkening sky.

This recognition runs deep in country practice: we came upon the foxhounds working along the undercliff, or, more exactly, we were attracted by the groups of watchers on the high tops crowning the cliffs and perilous escarpments. They were that motley of enthusiasts and wiseacres in stockings and britches, oiled jackets and flat 'ats, who occasionally whooped and pointed their thumb sticks as the foxes ran their endless circles round the islands of gorse and blackthorn. You certainly did not have to be a genius in fieldcraft to know that foxes were as thick on the ground as humans in a rush hour tube train.

The huntsman, hunting on foot, tried to keep his hounds on the line of one fox while three others skittered around fouling his scent. In one of those inevitable moments when the small pack was being whipped-in, the fox, a huge dog fox with an unusually large white tip to his brush and a white fleck on his shoulder, seen in as many moments as it takes a trotting fox to cover five yards of ground, was heading back to his original place of finding. Hunting foxes in this beautiful but impossible terrain is hardly more than an elaborate game which tires the followers, exercises the hounds and, from the short distance the fox keeps from the hounds, seems to bother him but very little. But that was "the huntsman's fox." "My fox," he declared, "I recognised him . . ." And having seen his old adversary once he would chase no other. This he did, all the long day, until we all went home to tea . . . the fox included.

Then something happened which is guaranteed to put all field naturalists in their place. We tend to be a race of knowalls deserving of being brought down to earth occasionally as when the impossible, the least expected, happens, and it happened to me. Some miles from the nearest river an otter bounded, in that unique arched-back fashion, across the road in my headlights.

I doubt whether anyone would have guessed there was an otter within thirty miles or more. They would have said there was not enough water and what there was would be too polluted. Otters have characteristics and personalities of total individuality, and I decided there and then that I would find out more about that otter and any others around my area and you might just as well know the end of the story now: from that day to this I never saw another otter there or anywhere else.

There is nothing unusual about that. Even "professional" otter watchers rarely see otters and many of their observations are based on the circumstantial evidence of food leftovers, resting places, breeding holts and their distinctive spraints. Then, for all the accumulated knowledge available, there is still considerable misunderstanding of the supposed conflict between otters and feral mink, and what can only be described as "a conspiracy of emotion" which led to the banning of otter hunting in Britain.

Let me make it quite clear that I do not support or condemn otter hunting but in this case, call it a field sport if you wish or see it as an archetypal game which the British are so good at inventing with uniforms (team colours), arcane rules (there is no silly mid-on or short square leg in otter hunting, but the whippers-in are the deep field players), thieves' Latin to mask the game and keep outsiders outside ... but in the end those who knew more about otters than a very small number of devoted biologists were the local otter hunters. And when we lost their contribution to conservation we all lost centuries of knowledge, experience and lore to no beneficial purpose.

There crept into my mind those prophetic words from Eliot's *Murder in the Cathedral*:

Now is my way clear, now is the meaning plain:
Temptation shall not come in this kind again.
The last temptation is the greatest treason:
To do the right deed for the wrong reason.

Let us look at the whole story and ask, whatever happened to the otter?

First of all we have to throw away some well-fed illusions about otters and mink because they cloud the true issue, and because mink colonisation has not yet reached saturation and may not do so for several decades. Even so, mink are so well established that nothing short of a national epidemic on the scale of myxomatosis or constant persecution such as that on coypu (forty years on there are still coypu in East Anglia) will now come close to eradicating these animals.

There are two very simple reasons why mink have been so successful in Britain: they are only semi-aquatic but they are completely catholic carnivores. The destruction they cause amongst wild and ornamental ducks and ducklings, ducks on their nests, Coots, Moorhen or the massacre they cause amongst ground nesting birds such as colonies of Shelduck, has to be seen to be believed. They even creep into the nesting holes of harmless kingfishers so that in a few nights a domestic pond or a small natural lake can be cleared of all its ground nesting, wading or water-borne birds.

Like inept criminals they scatter many clues: they devastated the Dutch coot population, which migrates in very cold winters to the lagoons behind the Chesil bank on the Dorset coast, leaving behind the ringed feet of their prey.

But there is also the irrefutable factor that mink occupy an ecological niche in Britain which, probably since before the last ice age eliminated moose, bears and ox and some smaller predatory animals, had never previously been occupied in Britain.

We should also dispel the old wives' tales of mink driving otters from their territories. On the evidence of our own eyes this is most unlikely. The otter diet is ninety per cent fish which accounts for only five per cent of mink diet. There is no true feeding conflict, and physical conflict is even less likely as the otter is more than twice the body weight of a mink and can be vicious and courageous in protecting its own interests.

But before our love affair with the otter gets out of hand it might be worth remembering that in exceptionally cold weather they have been known to take fully grown hares in the form and even weakling lambs, and they are sufficiently versatile to fish under ice like seals. And so the contradictions continue: otter watchers in Dorset discovered that where mink and otter share a territory it is usually the mink which graciously moves out when an otter moves in . . . not a case of survival of the fitter but survival of the stronger. But what is equally puzzling is that otter bitches prefer not to breed in mink territory and being very mobile prefer to travel to new water. The question is this, does the bitch ever return or does the dog otter follow her out of potential conflict?

This pattern of behaviour also illustrates two other parts of the mystery of otters in Britain: the otter is on the fringe of its geographic range in terms of climate and habitat and has historically had population densities lower than the five other major otter countries of western Europe, and they demand much greater areas of completely undisturbed territory and water than was ever previously believed. A dog otter will usually have a territory overlapping that of two bitches and may extend to twenty square kilometres and up to thirty kilometres length of river, although those being released from Philip Wayre's East Anglian otter sanctuary are being re-established on eight miles of carefully chosen unpolluted and undisturbed river.

That is the background to the story: trying to unravel what subsequently happened to the otter in post war years is closer to Agatha Christie than a conventional study of wildlife with clues, misleading clues, half truths and hysterics used to mislead the unwary, and downright lies to achieve dubious ends.

It is interesting, even to those who have never in their lives seen an otter in the wild, to follow the murky post war history not simply to see what happened to this beautiful and graceful creature but to learn to what lengths so-called conservationists will go to protect species, supposedly on our behalf. Whatever else is remembered or forgotten, mink are a wholly destructive naturalised species out of natural context in the British ecology, while the otter has always historically been in complete harmony with its world.

First, there were two major postwar otter surveys, largely based on information from hunts. The late Earl of Cranford, one of Britain's most knowledgeable and respected experts on otters and a keen protectionist, pointed out that having accepted the hunts' initial statistics — no one over-contradicted them because no one was then reasonably able to do so — protectionists then refused to accept any further hunt information on the spurious grounds that the source was, by definition, tainted.

The Otter Committee of the Mammal Society, in an independent assessment of the facts available, said that the cumulative effect of otter hunting, based on a steady level of the known location of individual otters and the numbers killed by hunts over a period of fifty-seven years was negligible on the total population. I need hardly add that the Mammal Society is not likely to trim its opinions to suit the vagaries of fashionable argument.

But in order to meet noisy public demands, otter hunting became otter dragging in which otters were hunted in their natual habitat but not killed. But by the mid 1960s the hunts themselves were beginning to report a rapid decline in otter numbers. Equally, naturalists in other otter territories reported no change, underlying the difficulties of making precise statements short of lengthy scientific surveys of populations anywhere.

But there was no doubt in anyone's mind: something was going wrong, very badly wrong . . . and one of the principal culprits, hunting, had already been eliminated.

Fortunately the murderer was soon found, but not easily dealt with. The greatest fall in the numbers of otters had occurred in those areas where persistent organochlorines such as Dieldrin and Aldrin were commonly used in sheep dips and seed dressings. The otter became just another statistic in a wholesale massacre which included tens of millions of songbirds, a whole range of raptors and scavengers at the peak of the food chain, more foxes in a year than were killed by hunting in a lifetime, and uncounted waterfowl.

The effect on otter populations was quickly seen to be catastrophic: otters were not to be seen in the countryside because the parents had been made infertile through eating fish which contained in their tissues high residuals of organochlorines from pesticides which had leached from farmland into almost every river and stream, however small, in agricultural Britain. Lord Cranbrook said that in the years 1960-7 no cohorts of sub-adults joined the population in the majority of breeding areas in England. The effect in only ten years was a decline in the population of forty per cent which led, in many places, to what are now only remnant populations probably insufficiently large to be self-perpetuating.

Then came a new twist in this already deceitful game: Lord Cranbrook, who introduced an otter protection bill to parliament suggested that the evidence used to secure the Bill through the House was wrong, even though the outcome was right:

". . . To do the right thing for the wrong reason"?

It was, quite simply, morally wrong to do so and as a new rule in the game of conservation created a hideously dangerous precedent. It is now difficult to condemn the animal rights activists for their ignorance, thuggery and violence when they have the noble Lord's precedent on which to base their anti-social activities. Indeed, unless conservation and those who practise it base their work on a profound and just moral philosophy it will fail. Worse, the conservationists and field naturalists, not synonymous interests, may themselves become corrupt.

Sometimes it is difficult enough to remember the real world in which we live: where a supposedly educated person can achieve, however briefly, national newspaper acceptance for the view that the nursery rhyme "Three Blind Mice" is a slur on mice and therefore unnecessarily cruel; where anti-vivisectionists (or "Animal Liberationists") can hurl petrol bombs at the home of a learned scientist but equally will ignore the fact that seventy otters each year are drowned in coastal stake nets in Scotland, representing a death toll 1,000 per cent higher than the largest number ever killed in a season's hunting, and also choose to take no practical action against an oil slick in the Shetlands which in a single night killed twenty otters. What haunts me, perhaps now on long reflection even angers me, is that the British experience of banning otter hunting may be carried on a wave of emotional hysteria to "protect" other species regardless of all the surrounding consequences of such an action. The next ban may well chip away another protective layer over the British countryside.

Because of the cumulative decline in the numbers of otters it would be well nigh impossible to make a case for the reintroduction of hunting but we have to remember Lord Cranford's ominous words, as a protectionist, when he claimed that the otter was not the verge of extinction at the time when hunting was banned and that otters did have a future in the UK: "One does not expect propaganda bodies which can have no pretensions to scientific objectivity or scientific integrity to be too nice about the evidence they seek to quote".

There are other games, no less arcane, no less Byzantine in their complexity but infinitely more enjoyable, and which draw out not only the better side of our natures but that gentle subtleness in the British character which makes life in the contryside so agreeable to the British and such a mystery to all foreigners. Which other nation invents a game to inflate pomposity for the sole purpose of publicly deflating it to the discomfort of the pompous?

The truth is self-revealing: we British are a strange race. We take national pride in appearing to do things badly and there is no better illustration of this than village sports.

Driving to Kirtlington in Oxfordshire, I glimpsed a village green cricket match. I had to stop. It was a compulsion . . . to watch complete strangers play just a couple of overs. Sometimes those two overs stretch to half a hundred and the afternoon has quietly slipped out of my grasp. Village cricket is as compulsive to me as drugs to an addict. But I wouldn't give you a single penny for a test match.

As I stood in the golden sunlight, ankle deep in ripe grasses, amid a vivid scattering of yarrow and rocket I realised, with blinding clarity, that not only do we like to do things badly, we like to be seen to do them badly. It is a public assertion of our amateur status.

And I have seen some cricket which was not just bad, but near farcical in its incompetence.

A late friend of mine, Marcus Feakes, possibly the nation's most mediocre cricketer and an actor whose performances were instantly forgettable, often fielded at deep third man on the slope at the Station Road end of St Helens Green. He could not see the game and the other players could not see him. It was an undeserved purdah for a man of his enthusiasms.

But he got his own back for his indignity. Following the game by ear he could anticipate when the ball was coming his way. He would then carefully roll the ball in a fresh cow pat, pick it up by the seam and throw it back into the unsuspecting fielder's hands.

At Toulston, in north Yorkshire, they play a form of village green polo, sometimes two a-side, sometimes three, but with full scale games on Sundays. There are some fine silver pots to be won in Yorkshire and teams come from far and wide to play on that sylvan field.

One player, by no means a young man said: "I milked eighty cows this morning; I am playing four chukkas of polo now and I'll milk eighty this evening". Was this not the reiteration of amateur status masking both skill and dedication with the modesty which comes from total confidence?

But why do we take such extraordinary pride in it? Is it inverted snobbery? The more professional we become the more we wish to shrug it off. We even apologise to each other for being good at our chosen jobs. We seem to be slightly ashamed. Oddly enough this seems to apply least to artisan and skilled manual jobs where men take just pride in their work — you can see it on their faces, that smile of contentment at a positive achievement.

But they are not ashamed in their ability in country pubs. I stopped overnight near Launceston where "Devil Amongst the Tailors" was being played in the pub. To grasps of appreciation from his friends the local star player relieved me of several pounds in incautious bets. Of course, he let me win the first two games, lulled me into that false sense of security before he pounced.

Travelling on I arrived at the Tinners Arms at Zennor where the grinding of the sea on granite cliffs in an October gale can be heard inside the pub, and a one-eyed septuagenarian and a man with one arm beat me easily at darts . . . to the amusement of their friends.

So what chance would I have with "Nine Men's Morris" (Merels) when my young daughter beat me three times in a row, or in a game of skill and accuracy such as "Aunt Sally". Recollection of my playing pub skittles in Somerset many years ago is still regarded as an intrusion into private grief in this family.

In Kent, by the way, "Devil Amongst the Tailors" is called "Daddlums", meaning "unsteady". I have often wondered if the meaning is the same as the affectionate nickname, "Diddlums", used in the Isle of Wight.

As the seasons change the amateur appears in other sports. As the "flannelled fools" leave the field, the "muddied oafs" come on — men in their forties scrumming down with the lads, downing their pints in the club house afterwards and bellowing bawdy songs; men of almost fifty kicking soccer balls around our field while the horses stand on the touch line and ponder on the wisdom of man; men who ought to, and do, know better risking their necks in the mad chase over point-to-point fences. But you cannot stop them, can you? And if you did they would only find something else equally dangerous to do.

Such thoughts of winter cold and mud give way as a slow procession of almost oriental colour and dignity leaves the New Inn — it was "New" at the time of William and Mary when the houses surrounding the green were built — the men in their whites, the women rippling in pastel frocks and under wide hats. The men stand about the wicket, the women set out their canvas chairs and their picnic baskets under the vast limes whose seeds are beginning to ripen. I am already looking forward to afternoon tea on the boundary, the ultimate deft touch of civilisation in rural England.

There is a contradiction: the men who should be the peacocks and who are already showing off at the wicket look plain by comparison with the wives and girlfriends chattering in circles near the scoreboard.

Then you realise that the men are only showing off to each other. The spectators on the boundary do not matter, they are ornaments to the game, not participants. Perhaps that is the secret of the game of which I am the only spectator living up to his name. The ladies are sipping Pimms; the ice is tinkling into glasses . . . even the scorer has spreadeagled himself in the spears of couch and ryegrass. His girlfriend nudges him when something happens on the field, but it is an idiosyncratic rather than an accurate record of a match which is truly . . .

But the ultimate contradiction is that the Village Championship finals is played at Lords. What, I ask, is wrong with St Helens Green? Has anyone ever found a more beautiful pitch than Steephill?

But there is worse to come. Reports of the Lords' game used wild adjectives such as "gallant" and "surprise triumph".

They do not use strong language like that down here among the yarrow where a fielder is thrashing about in a vast clump of bearded rose-bay willow herb looking for a lost ball.

Why, it would almost be an insult, wouldn't it. They play bad cricket down here and they are proud of it.

I was going to add, "At the other end of the scale . . ." but in sport there are no scales; differences yes, degrees of passion which we put into our sports; differences in what we take out of our involvements.

That difference is expressed to an almost exaggerated extent in one of the most beautiful, almost balletic, complex but simple and far away one of the most dangerous and most expensive sports invented by man: high goal polo.

Even during the worst years of unemployment, when companies were failing faster than New Year resolutions and even public houses were threatening to close because there was no money with which to drown our sorrows, there were more men, and a scattering of women, playing polo from the heady social atmosphere of Smith's Lawn at Windsor, before half the royal family, to those delightful country pitches where the game itself is the only first amongst equals.

While the nation was flexing its muscles to find a new internal economic dynamism polo clubs were putting up their fees, not to maintain their financial sinews but to dissuade potential members. Even so they failed to stem the flood of applicants to whom the thick end of £1,000 for a five month season is no deterrent whatsoever.

These new players fit a new pattern. Almost without exception they are what we used to call entrepreneurs and capitalists before the words became scorned, men in their mid thirties able to devolve management of their own companies to responsible deputies mid-week when arduous practice chukkas are played and the league matches of tournaments are battled out. They are the men who run the small businesses, partnerships and industries. They are not the elected directors of public companies, restrained by formalised disciplines of the commercial world. Others again are doctors, dentists, engineers rather than the aristocratic army officers and the maharajas whose timid ghosts probably haunt Hurlingham to this day.

The regeneration of this classic game is characterised in another way which is clear to see: self confidence. There are only two truths in polo: you can either play the game or you can't, and if you can't you are cruelly exposed in the first few seconds of the game; the second is that polo is not a game for people who need to make excuses. That is why the new men populating our country polo pitches — and their wives and girlfriends who have taken up the game because they are no longer willing to wait decoratively on club lawns and watch when they can play equally well on their husband's or boyfriend's ponies — are innovators, not inheritors.

Theirs is a public display of success when, too often, it seems that half the nation is paw-mouthing its failures and blaming everyone except themselves for their own inadequacies. The man who has earned himself a comfortable home, won himself an attractive bride, can afford to send his children to the school of his choice, not the choice of the man in the town hall or the political ideologue in the council chamber, deserves to express his social muscle in this way.

Over the years I have noticed one basic characteristic in naturalists: for all their outbursts of noise and gregariousness they are, inside, solitary people, people who are happy, perhaps at their happiest, in the long hours of their own company and as far away from everyone else as they can get.

A friend says jokingly, at least I think he was joking, "If I can see my neighbour he is too close; if I can hear him it's total war". Even now, after half a lifetime, I still regard, wholly unjustly, the approach of a stranger in the country with only half concealed hostility . . . but do not make the mistake of believing that the most obvious place is necessarily the most solitary. I put the question to you: have you ever seen ten thousand umbrellas under the sea; white ones, fully opened and silvered with fractured sun shining down on them?

This wild, surreal vision keeps flying back to my mind because at an age when most men are reaching for their golf clubs and anicipating the juniper flavoured delights at the nineteenth hole, I went back to the silent world.

The coast where I swim runs from safe sands where Lewis Carroll and Alice made sandcastles to cliffs tormented by seas which endlessly pound on huge rocks as romantic as the Big Sur or the coast of Maine and which inspired writers from the ailing Keats to Swinburne, Chesterton and De Vere.

Further on Tennyson in black wideawake and flowing cloak stalked sheep-cropped downs, which now bear his name, over bays where today sail-boarders skittle from wave top to wave top and beach boys ride the surf.

But at half tides there are sheltered lagoons between rock ledges which drop, reputedly seven fold, into the English Channel.

This is a world upside down, a pretended facsimile of what we arrogantly believe is the real world. Here are meadows, deserts of shimmering sand, forests of tall weed in a hundred shades of autumn which bend not to the wind but in silent response to the waves above; wastes of brown rock sometimes decorated with garish, animal flowers and a bustling, teeming population of rainbow colours never seen on land.

I set my orange marker buoy on a small anchor. If you are swimming alone it is best that someone responsible knows where you are ... even if you do not want them to join you. It is said that there is the wreck of a schooner below Sharpass Rocks. The pathless way to it is through a vast forest of stemmed brown weed. This is a strange world: up there on the cliff tops most people know the names of a few wild flowers, some grasses and trees, a handful of birds. But down here every plant is a new-found mystery and not one person in a million seems to know the names of these unfamiliar seaweeds, the anemones, the hosts of tiny fish, not even the professional fishermen who have spent their lives on the beach and coastal waters.

Technicolour wrasse hover like hummingbirds on the edge of my forest; I am confronted by the dull, passionless eyes and gaping mouth of the biggest sea bass I have ever seen. Now, if I had a harpoon ... but with one scarcely energetic twist of his tail he has gone and I see him watching with the same disinterest twenty feet away but still half concealed in the forest. But I carry only a weighted broom handle with a spike for poking around on my estate.

I never found the schooner. It probably broke up decades ago, but I find a sea bed strewn with lumps of coal, and where the ledge falls into deep water a cargo of roadstone granite from Cornwall gleams like silver dust from yet another long-forgotten grounding.

A few hundred yards out are the tangled steel plates of the *Empress Queen*, a troopship which ran aground in 1917. The crew were saved and a score of soldiers stayed briefly at our farmhouse. Perhaps this is now their only memorial, we shall never know.

There my affinity with the ship ends. Currents whirl by in impatient patterns which seem to change by the minute and chunks of metal, sharpened by the erosion of the sea, remind me, however illogically, of the pendulum in Edgar Allen Poe's "Pit".

This sets off a train of thought that I know of no poetry written about the world beneath the sea. Tennyson's waves are still breaking on cold grey stones and the salt-caked smoke-stacks still huddle in the bay from the south-westerlies except that today they are likely to be trawlers flying Norwegian and Soviet flags as much as the "dirty British coasters" which these days are gleamingly clean.

But there are moments of fairy-tale beneath the waves. Swimming over a patch of barren silver sand in filtered sunlight I thought of all the good reasons why it should not hold any aquatic life until I noticed the perfect outline of a plaice, precise to its peripheral fins, dusted with sand, his stalked eyes protruding above the camouflage. He was watching me as closely as I was watching him. So I gave him a prod and he shot away for only a few feet where he shimmied into the sand again, still watching.

Then there is the grandfather of all lobsters standing on his front doorstep taking on the passing world with his twitching whiskers, and the day an exquisite mermaid with aqualung and black shining diving suit popped out of the forest, her blond hair streaming through the tinted water. She smiled and waved, as tempting a siren as I shall ever see below the waves, except that she was followed by Poseidon himself in the form of a blond-bearded viking who carried a harpoon and neither smiled nor waved as he disappeared into the forest with the girl. Ah well, dreams are cheap enough.

One afternoon, within hearing of the children shrieking and splashing in the warm rock pools, I was intrigued by lines of exact demarcation as clear as the walls of a house where a current of warm water surged through noticeably colder water so that I could reach out from the warm into the cold at the stretch of an arm. Then I saw above me — I was about twenty feet down — a sight which at first filled me with primitive fear; ten thousand, perhaps a hundred thousand . . . half a million, numbers beyond estimate of silvery translucent umbrellas with flexible multiple handles being borne along by the warm current. Jelly fish, all six to nine inches across, all marked with purple circles, opening and closing like gently clenching fists, all tilted at an angle in the direction in which they were heading. Twenty feet deep of them and forty feet wide of them, soup plate to soup plate of them and all seemingly going on forever as far as I could see, and then beyond through the clear water, an insane, fevered surreal vision of unique and harmless beauty.

At first I swam cautiously among them, swishing them away like undersea thistledown, swam with them, against them and through them, allowing them to bounce off my body and twist helplessly through the water setting up multiple collisions; and still they came, powerless to resist the destiny of a slow moving current of warm water.

Those are the visions, the unwritten undersea poems of umbrellas beneath the waves and real, smiling mermaids — I never saw the mermaid or the sea god again — which urges me to maintain my kit meticulously in the glamourless world of a garage on a bleak winter night.

When illusion and reality combine it is the perfect dream.

ISIS publish a wide range of books in large print, from fiction to biography. Any suggestions for books you would like to see in large print or audio are always welcome. Please send to the Editorial department at:

ISIS Publishing Ltd.
7 Centremead
Osney Mead
Oxford OX2 0ES
(01865) 250 333

A full list of titles is available free of charge from:
Ulverscroft large print books

(UK)
The Green
Bradgate Road, Anstey
Leicester LE7 7FU
Tel: (0116) 236 4325

(Australia)
P.O Box 953
Crows Nest
NSW 1585
Tel: (02) 9436 2622

(USA)
1881 Ridge Road
P.O Box 1230, West Seneca,
N.Y. 14224-1230
Tel: (716) 674 4270

(Canada)
P.O Box 80038
Burlington
Ontario L7L 6B1
Tel: (905) 637 8734

(New Zealand)
P.O Box 456
Feilding
Tel: (06) 323 6828

Details of **ISIS** complete and unabridged audio books are also available from these offices. Alternatively, contact your local library for details of their collection of **ISIS** large print and unabridged audio books.